# THE GUIDE TO HEALING FROM PAST TRAUMA

Real-World, Personally Tested Strategies
To Heal Your PTSD, Calm Your Nervous System
& Regulate Your Emotions

Information For All Readers

This text discusses important life events, psychological concepts and mental health issues. The work has been checked for accuracy and relevance by licensed health care professionals. However, you should remain aware that this text does not act as a substitute for therapy nor should you rely on the content of this book as your sole means of therapeutic relief. You are advised to seek the input of licensed mental health experts who can make a proper diagnosis having regard for your unique circumstances.

Stories throughout this text contain detailed information about traumatic events. These stories may cause some readers to become distressed. Readers, please be mindful of this as you proceed. Such stories are presented at the start of each chapter. If you skip these stories your understanding of the concepts in the book will not be undermined.

*We're led by God. Our business is also committed to supporting kids' charities. At the time of printing, we have donated well over $100,000 to enable mentoring services for underprivileged children. By choosing our books, you are helping children who desperately need it. Thank you.*

## This is really important.
## It's a sincere thank you.

My name is Wayne, the founder of LearnWell.

My Dad put a book in my hands when I was 13. It was written by Zig Ziglar and it changed the course of my life. Since then, it's been books that have helped me get over breakups, learn how to be a good friend, study the lives of good people and books have been the source of my persistence through some pretty challenging times.

My purpose is now to return the favor. To create books that might be the turning point in the lives of people around the world, just like they've been for me. It's enough to almost bring me to tears to think of you holding this book, seeking information and wisdom from something that I've helped to create. I'm moved in a way that I can't fully explain.

We're a small and 'beyond-enthusiastic' team here at LearnWell. We're writers, editors, researchers, designers, formatters (oh ... and a bookkeeper!) who take your decision to learn with us incredibly seriously. We consider it a privilege to be part of your learning journey. Thank you for allowing us to join you.

If there's anything we did really well, anything we messed up, or anything AT ALL that we could do better, would you please write to us and tell us (like, right now!) We would love to hear from you!

readers@learnwellbooks.com

We're sending you our thanks, our love and our very best wishes.

*Wayne*

and the team at LearnWell Books.

# WELCOME TO OUR
# COMMUNITY

## "It's like a private online book club"

 Imagine if you could actually meet and talk with other readers of this book and share your experiences.

 Imagine if you could chat with the author or join them on a live Q&A!

 Imagine getting access to the author's notes and other exclusive, unpublished material.

**You can do all of that and a lot more in the LearnWell Online Community!!**

→ Download your **Workbook**

→ Chat directly with the author!

→ Meet and feel supported by other readers and their experiences.

→ Access additional, exclusive content about this topic and others.

→ Join our live Author Q&A sessions online.

→ Learn faster, make lasting changes, and have 10 times more fun!

**All of this is part of our commitment to creating the best learning resources in the world.**

**Scan the QR code to get FREE access**

www.learnwellbooks.com/healed

# CO-AUTHOR

Our internal team of writers creates our books. We collaborate together, research together, edit each other's manuscripts, and collectively take responsibility for the written work we produce.

Sometimes we will seek input from a subject matter expert who can add meaningful insight on a topic. We interview that expert, often adopt their tone and style and refer to them in the first person. On this occasion, we worked with ...

## Greg Sara

Greg was born in Adelaide, Australia in 1971. 'Colorful' would be a very mild way to describe his life. He's lived everywhere from Europe to China and the Middle East. He's performed as a DJ at clubs, festivals, and parties all over the world. He's been an event manager, film producer, landscaper, an absolute hero, a nobody, and to those around him, without fail, a very good friend.

Greg has fought life-threatening addictions to drugs and alcohol and he has suffered time staring at the pit of existence and had his own near-death moments. More than once. All of which are an extension of his childhood trauma. From deep, dark places, with the help of very special people along the way, Greg has discovered the unpaved path back to health, joy, and a life of true contribution. His personal experience of healing is borderline miraculous and a lesson for those with whom he shares his vivid, gritty, very personal story. His wish is that this story might be the cause of others' own healing.

Greg now lives in Queensland, Australia, and can most frequently be found swimming in cold water, well before the sun comes up.

**To Nick**

I wish I knew this while you were still here.

# CONTENTS

# YOUR
# WORKBOOK

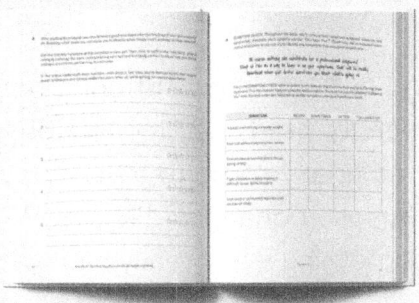

A shocking truth was discovered by a study done in 1987 – **people only remember 10% of what they read!**

That seems so discouraging.

But here's the **GOOD NEWS** – reading is **NEVER** a waste of time. As long as you do **one** important thing …

The same study (by National Training Laboratories) shows that you will remember 90% of what you read when you **put your new knowledge into action!**

Here at LearnWell, we aim to create **the world's best learning resources**. So, we have included a highly engaging **Workbook** that helps you put your new knowledge into fun, practical action.

So, make sure you download your **FREE Workbook.** You'll find it located inside the **LearnWell Community.** Simply scan the QR code below for access.

**Get your Workbook in the LearnWell Community**
Scan the QR Code for access or go to:
www.learnwellbooks.com/healed

# INTRODUCTION

When I think back, there were many moments that should have been my wake-up calls, but they weren't loud enough for me to pay attention. It wasn't until I found myself laid out on a bathroom floor, barely conscious, vomiting up blood, that I knew it was time to "wake up".

It was near the end of 2021. I was suffering major burnout from overworking. 30 years of drug and alcohol abuse, and everything I'd been through had finally come to a head. My body was telling me I had to make some changes, like, NOW! It was a simple choice. If I didn't, something really, really bad was going to happen.

I knew a lot of my behavior to this point had stemmed from past trauma. The addiction, the people pleasing, the hyperfunctioning. It's frighteningly common among adults, especially in this post-Covid world. It's estimated that 70% of people in America have been through a traumatic event. That's over 223 million people[1]. While most people will be able to recover from their traumatic experiences, many will develop some form of post-traumatic stress disorder or PTSD. In 2020, around 13 million Americans had PTSD, and it's estimated that 5% of the population will have PTSD at any given time[2].

The signs were all there. The flashbacks. The dramatic mood swings. The insomnia. The emotional outbursts. The self-blame and recriminations. The heart palpitations. The fear. The depression. The anxiety. All of these and more were my constant companions for which I constantly self–medicated in some way shape or form. My PTSD was like that annoying little brother who makes your life miserable, but unlike a little brother who will eventually grow out of it, I felt like I was stuck with this painful intruder.

No. I just couldn't accept that. I couldn't live like that. I was not going to be tormented for the rest of my life. I wasn't going to be a victim. I knew there had to be a way to overcome this. To stand up to this relentless mental bullying.

My journey to recovery wasn't easy. There were days I would cry continuously. Although I was hurting so much, I couldn't make a sound. I was so afraid of the noise my pain would make that I couldn't let it out. In my mind, that scream would have sounded like murder. A sound from a place so dark that I didn't want anyone to hear it.

I can't tell you where it all started, but I know it began at an early age. A good place to start would probably be Christmas 1981 when I was hit by a car on my brand new BMX. The impact pretty much tore my right leg off. The sound brought a large gathering to the street, one of whom happened to be an emergency ward nurse. She plugged my bleeding femoral artery with a ballpoint pen and held it there until the ambulance arrived. They said on the way to hospital that if she hadn't done that I would have bled out well before they got there. On arrival at the hospital, the doctors on staff said that they were going to have to remove my leg. It was only by coincidence that a bone healing specialist from Canada was walking past and saw my hysterical mother in the hallway. He offered to operate on me and the next morning I came out of surgery, leg intact. I spent 3 months in traction, another 6 months in plaster from the chest down and another 6 months in a caliper once the cast was removed. I was too young to tell, but I'm pretty sure I went a little insane during this period.

Next up was my parents. They both loved me dearly, but they had a passionate and toxic relationship. Open the dictionary to 'narcissist' and you'd see a picture of my father. He would verbally and emotionally abuse my mother, which was horrifying to watch. As an only child, there was nowhere to hide, no one to crawl into a blanket fort with. I felt alone, utterly hopeless and helpless.

They were both in the travel industry, so I used to travel a lot growing up. It gave me some respite, but when they were both home, they used to fight. A lot. They separated several times, but always found their way back to each other. In my immature mind, I had no clue what was going on. Was this love? Was this what a normal family was meant to be like? I was happy when my father left because it meant I had a break from the screaming and the arguments.

As a child, we trust our parents to know what to do for the best. But what my parents were doing just didn't feel right.

When I was 15, my father had moved out. Finally! Now Mum and I could live in peace. One night some time after their separation, I remember he came over to our house, I don't recall why but there he was, standing, screaming through the flyscreen door and he and I ended up physically fighting.

I'd had enough. I wanted him to feel some of the pain that he had put us through. I thought we were free of his bullying and here he was, waltzing back into our lives, still thinking he could treat us like dirt. Years and years of listening to my parents arguing had taken its toll. When I saw that same pattern of behavior unfolding yet again I lost it. My temper exploded and I lashed out, wanting nothing more than to teach my father a lesson.

That incident triggered a downward spiral which led me to depressive episodes and self harming. Then from about 19 years of age I started working in the music industry and that self harm descended into heavy alcohol and drug abuse. My upbringing had left me with a hefty dose of self-hatred and abandonment issues which pursued me until my late 20s. That's when I realized I had a problem. I needed help and people around me who could support me while I worked things through. However, the music industry back then wasn't known for its clean living. The inner work I was doing was offset by partying all the time. I never really gave myself the space to dig deep into my issues or do any real healing. It's hard to heal when you're high all the time.

Eventually I found myself working as a producer in an advertising agency. I was heavily overworked, overcompensating for my problem with people pleasing and kidding myself that if I was successful that would finally make me happy.

Instead I became really sick. Then, during Covid, as was the case for so many of us in the creative fields, my income had fallen through the floor. My roommate and I set up an Italian food business and would make pasta and soup for our friends to give us some purpose and a bit of extra cash. One night, a friend of mine who I hadn't seen in ages came over to pick up some soup. I'll call her Anna. As she walked through my front door she turned and looked at me and said "Are you okay, Greg?"

Normally, I would have brushed her off with a shrug and casual "I'm fine" but I was worn out.

"I'm really not ok right now …"

*We all need someone who will do this for us*

13

Taken by my vulnerability, she told me she was going for an ice bath the next day and invited me to go with her. I'd been promising myself that I was going to try one and had been putting it off forever and thought it's now or never.

I'd always hated the cold growing up. If a pool wasn't heated, you weren't going to get me in it. Under normal circumstances, there was no way Anna would have been able to persuade me to go near the water, but my circumstances were far from normal.

Getting into that water was a real shock to the system. It felt like all the air left my lungs as I got into the water and I questioned why anyone would want to do this to themselves. Yet when I got out, I noticed some massive shifts in my mood. I felt calmer, focused, but more importantly, *alive*. I could swear my eyesight was better.

I started taking regular ice baths and noticed that I felt so much better on the days I submerged myself in the freezing water. I did some research into why this might be and discovered that hydrotherapy was far from new. As far back as the ancient Greeks, Hippocrates was recommending hydrotherapy to treat mental illness.[3] In the 1800s, the Germans popularized hydrotherapy using cold water to treat various conditions.[4] More recently, Wim Hof has been teaching how cold exposure and breathing techniques can provide relief for many maladies - including PTSD.[5]

When I found out that there was scientific evidence to support ice baths[6], I began to wonder what other alternative therapies might be able to help. I decided I needed to truly focus on myself for the first time in my life. So when Anna invited me to join her at a breathwork session, I did and found that it built on the sense of inner harmony I was getting from my ice baths. I loved how taking time out to simply be with my breath enabled me to press pause on the restless busyness of my mind.

Anna, who had recently decided to set herself up as a life coach, became one of the most important people along my road to healing. Just her encouragement to take these first early steps had helped me so much, I was keen to see what else she could do. Together, we established a morning routine which supported my mental health.

With her help I could feel myself changing. I started consistently showing up for myself. I went back to therapy. I did EMDR (Eye Movement Desensitization and Processing) and IFS (Internal Family Systems) which I had a lot of really good results with.

My journey had begun. I explored so many methods and modalities. I experimented and took risks. I ventured well away from where I felt comfortable, seeking out resistance in myself wherever I could find it. Well away from the safe space where I and all of my issues had made a home for so many years. That work and those experiences have brought me to this moment. Where I now get to share my journey with you.

This book is for anyone else who is suffering because of the traumatic events they've lived through. I've been stunned to discover just how many of us there are, many of which you can find in the LearnWell Community, and it breaks my heart to think of so many people struggling the way I did. I know that what I'm going to tell you in this book works. I'm living proof that it does.

I've transformed from a self-harming addict, an alcoholic who almost died from the stomach ulcer that I created by pushing the boundaries of work, drugs and alcohol too far, to waking up every morning filled with excitement about what the day may bring. Gone is the self-loathing that was my permanent companion. I no longer punish myself for the things I went through that weren't my fault. I've been able to put the past in its proper context. It no longer has any hold over me. I get to choose my own destiny. Sure I still have my moments, but for the first time in my life, I feel like I'm the one driving.

So let me be your guide. I'll share all that I've learnt. I'll show you the path that I've walked. I'll point to all the potholes. I'll hold your hand as we traverse the scary parts and I'll support you when it feels too steep to take another step.

We'll start by discovering what trauma is and how it affects you. It may be that you experience symptoms you thought were just part of life. So, for example, you could learn that it's not actually normal to be constantly fatigued. That's your trauma draining you. Wouldn't it feel good to be overflowing with energy instead?

No, you don't have to feel guilty about what you went through. You are not to blame for other people's actions.

Yes, you *can* get a good night's sleep, one that's not troubled by nightmares or waking up feeling anxious for no apparent reason.

Yes, you *can* talk about what happened without getting tearful or distressed.

It's all possible. I promise.

The first part of this book will help you to understand what impact your trauma is having on your life. PTSD can cause permanent biological changes to the brain[7] but that doesn't mean you have to live with trauma symptoms for the rest of your life. I'm going to show you that you have the power to take back control. You don't have to let trauma rule you.

I'll also discuss the kind of experiences you'll have on your journey to trauma recovery. It won't always be "beer and discos". The road will be rocky at times. But when you know what to expect, you can put mechanisms in place to deal with the difficult sections of the path. You can minimize the challenges so you can activate your recovery faster.

I'll also show you some tools available to help deal with your trauma. FYI … this isn't a one size fits all process. What works for one trauma sufferer isn't necessarily a good fit for another. So I'm going to give you some options so you can choose the approach that suits you best.

Finally, I'll give you the blueprint you need to make permanent, healthy lifestyle changes which will make a massive difference to your trauma response.

Given you're reading this right now, I'll assume that you're not willing to allow your trauma to control your thoughts and your wellbeing any more.

On that basis, it's time to turn the page - literally and metaphorically.

Greg Sara

# PART 1

## Understanding

In this section we're going to talk about trauma, what it is, how it works, and why you're struggling to move past it. This will help you understand what's going on inside your mind so you can begin to undo the damage.

# 1

*You're not alone, my friend*

## WE'RE ALL HURTING

### The Trauma Epidemic

*Never compare yourself to anyone else. Everyone's struggle is different.*

## JOE'S STORY:

I was driving to work when another flashback hit me. The sensations were overwhelming. It was like I was right back in that moment when I was mugged at knifepoint. I could see the flash of the metal blade, smell the stench of my attacker's unwashed clothes as he snarled at me to hand over my wallet. I was only 15, I didn't carry much cash on me. When the mugger saw how little I had, he snarled again and drove the knife into my stomach. I felt a cold sensation as the metal plunged into me, then I was consumed by fiery agony. I collapsed, mercifully passing out to escape the pain.

Luckily, a passerby found me, before I lost too much blood, and called an ambulance. I missed the rest of that term of school. While I physically recovered within a few weeks, the mental scars remained.

Following that incident, I carried on with life and put on a brave show. On the surface it might have appeared that I was doing OK. I had a job, a girlfriend, and an active social life. But unknown to everyone, I was haunted by a crippling mental illness.

That mugging incident robbed me of any sense of safety. Nowhere was safe, not even my home. I'd been offered counseling while I was in hospital, but I turned it down. I didn't want to appear weak. Looking back, I wish I'd said yes. It would have made such a difference.

It took months before I could close my eyes without seeing my attacker's face. His unkempt beard. His shaggy eyebrows. His hazel eyes. He was there every time I tried to sleep.

I began obsessively checking all the windows, doors, and locks multiple times a day, convinced he'd come back to finish the job he'd started. I had panic attacks. School was impossible. My parents had to homeschool me. Somehow I managed to graduate high school, but my grades would have been so much better if I wasn't recovering from trauma. I went from one of the popular kids at school to a total recluse.

Over the years, my symptoms faded. I went to community college and got good grades. I managed to get into grad school and wound up working in finance. For a while, I was able to convince myself that I was fine. I was functional. I'd buried my ordeal in the depths of my memory.

It was a stupid movie that triggered the flashback. It included a scene with a mugging that wasn't even like what I experienced, but it was enough to ignite the memories. It was as if the intervening years hadn't happened. I was right back in the moment of the attack, only now I was haunted by images of someone attacking my girlfriend as well as myself. Violence taunted me every time I closed my eyes. I couldn't focus or concentrate. My job involved a lot of socializing, but I stopped going out. I couldn't face it. I lost accounts because of it. I knew my job was under threat, but it didn't matter. My panic attacks were making it impossible for me to leave the house anyway.

I did my best to keep it together, but it was like trying to resist the force of a wave.

Luckily for me, I had a boss who was understanding. She insisted I go see a therapist and they diagnosed me with PTSD. Knowing that my feelings were linked to a cause and that there were treatments available was such a relief.

I used a combination of medication and behavioral therapy to deal with the most severe symptoms of my PTSD. I took time off work and eventually decided not to go back. Instead my girlfriend and I are making plans to travel the world, something that would have been impossible before I got treatment.

While I don't know if I'll ever be fully cured from PTSD, I do have plenty of tools I can turn to so I don't suffer like I used to. I'm not a victim of my trauma any more. The right diagnosis and treatment weren't just life changing. They were life *saving*.

## WHAT IS TRAUMA?

The simple definition of trauma is that it is an emotional response to a difficult event. But that definition belies the reality of living with the condition. It also ignores that an event doesn't have to be massively traumatic to cause trauma. Many of us think that you only get PTSD if you go through a violent, dramatic event like warfare, extreme violence or a natural disaster. In fact, PTSD can be caused by a range of experiences, including accidents, attacks, childbirth, the loss of a loved one, childhood or domestic abuse, serious health issues, etc.

It's sad that there are very few of us who haven't experienced trauma in one form or another. Regardless of background or privilege, most of us have been through traumatizing events which have left their scars. Recognising that you have been traumatized is the first step toward healing. The first thing you have to do is not judge yourself against others. Your trauma is unique and doesn't care about other people's experiences. Trying to diminish how you feel by comparing yourself to other people you believe have been through worse isn't helpful and it's not going to heal you. Understand that however you feel is your reaction to what you've been through and everyone responds in their own way. There's no right or wrong, no one set way to react to trauma. Own your feelings and accept that it's okay for this to be your reaction. You are not a bad person. You are not weak. Even the strongest bones break under enough pressure. You are someone who has been through trauma and deserves healing *without* judgment - including from yourself.

## WHERE DOES TRAUMA BEGIN?

For many people, trauma goes right back to our childhood, possibly even in situations we can't remember. To paraphrase the wise poet Philip Larkin, *They mess you up, your mum and dad. They might not mean to, but they do.* I grew up in a disruptive family environment as an only child. A lot of the issues I'm dealing with today came from this environment. Today, children who have lived through the pandemic are at particular risk of trauma damage. These children were subjected to more violence than when schools were open. A Save the Children survey found that one in five caregivers admitted to being more negative or violent in their parenting methods. (And those were only the ones who were willing to be honest.)[1] Children and young people around the world struggled with their mental health due to stress, worry and a lack of social outlets. Online abuse increased at a time when more young people turned to technology to learn and maintain their friendships. Many families were driven into poverty because of the pandemic, a known factor in poor mental health.[2]

But it isn't all about your childhood. You may have had the best of childhoods and still suffer from trauma if you've been through a traumatic event. How much of an impact that will have depends on a number of factors and even then we still can't predict who will develop PTSD and who won't. Risk factors include:

- **Gender.** Women are twice as likely as men to develop PTSD

- **Genetics.** There is a link between PTSD and other inherited mental health conditions such as depression or schizophrenia.

- **Poor support system.** If you don't have a strong support network of family or friends, you're more likely to have a stronger reaction to trauma.

- **Pre-existing mental health conditions.** If you're already suffering with your mental health, say from anxiety, depression, or addiction, you have a greater chance of developing PTSD.[3]

## THE SYMPTOMS OF PTSD

There are four main categories of PTSD symptoms:

### Intrusive Thoughts

Unpredictable. Unwanted. Uninvited. Not even necessarily triggered by something. PTSD can bring with it flashbacks and nightmares that force you to relive your trauma again and again, as if it's happening right now.

## Negative Feelings

Emotions can be irrational. It doesn't matter how much you intellectually know you're not to blame for what happened to you, that doesn't stop the guilt and self-recrimination. You may find yourself feeling apathetic, detached and alienated from the world around you. This isolation can make your symptoms worse.

## Reactive Symptoms

Hypervigilance means you're constantly looking for threats around you. Again, you may well understand on a logical level that nothing bad's going to happen, but at the same time, the unexpected and unwanted has happened before. Why couldn't lightning strike twice? You could feel permanently stressed and irritable, which impacts on your quality of sleep or ability to get involved in commonplace activities.

## Avoidance

It's hardly surprising that trauma sufferers often don't like discussing what happened. But this goes deeper. It can make them stay away from places, things, or people that remind them of their experiences. So, for example, if you suffered medical trauma, this could make you avoid seeking medical care in the future, even if you really need it.

## And It Gets Worse...

So many of us accept our trauma as a simple fact of life when it doesn't need to be. This is exacerbated by so many aspects of modern living. Communities are fractured or even nonexistent, leaving us with a lack of support groups. Without someone to turn to, trauma can become amplified, worsening your symptoms. While being alone can have its benefits, it's crucial to have someone to talk to when you need to. I've been lucky to have a good support network at various points in my life and when I haven't I've turned to professional help. But not everyone has that luxury. Not everyone feels like they can talk about their experiences without putting themselves at even more risk of harm.

While we should be able to turn to our family at least, many of us don't have that supportive network to rely on. While some people can take family love for granted, when that's missing, it leaves a hole in our lives that trauma rushes to fill.

Social media is supposed to bring us all together, yet so often it drives a wedge between us. The internet connects us with people across the globe but many of us feel disconnected from our neighbors and community. We might inadvertently create echo chambers around ourselves, blocking those with differing opinions to our own if it becomes too overwhelming. Our self-worth gets caught up in the admiration of others. We compare how many likes and comments we get to our peers and feel a sense of failure or lack of acceptance if we don't measure up. We tell ourselves that we have a community around us because we have hundreds or even thousands of social media 'friends' and followers, but forget that we're missing a very important piece of that community - the transfer of energy human beings enjoy when we're in the same place together. You know that feeling when you spend an afternoon with your favourite person. You feel energised.

Through it all, we've lost sight of the one thing that could bring relief: peace. We've become so driven to buy things we don't need in the mistaken belief that it will make us happy. And if we're happy, we'll feel better, right? Well, not quite. Happiness is a fleeting emotion, just like any other. I always thought that being successful and constantly on the go would make me happy. Instead, it just made me busy and stressed. If you don't have peace in your soul, you'll never find contentment, no matter how hard you look for it.

It's only when we start to look inward and find self love that the real healing can start. We tend to look for something outside of ourselves to heal but rarely direct that energy to where it really needs to go - within. It's understandable. Right now, your mind is a scary place to be. But that can change.

First up, it's important to understand the extent of how your trauma has affected you. In the next chapter we'll look more at what you might be experiencing as a result of your trauma. This may be the explanation you finally need for what you've been going through.

 Before moving on to Chapter 2, turn now to your Workbook. There are activities in there that make your healing journey personal and unique to you. Do that now and get in the habit of taking a pause at the end of each chapter to draw the benefit from what's contained in the Workbook.

# HOW TRAUMA
# CAN HURT US

Why The Damage From Trauma
Lingers Long After The Trigger Event

*Although the world is full of suffering,*
*it is also full of the overcoming of it.*

*– Helen Keller*

## MARIE'S STORY:

Most people know what a flashback is when it comes to PTSD. You see it in movies all the time. A character who's been through a difficult experience will suddenly see it pass before their eyes, reliving it as though it was happening right now.

Not so many people know about PTSD body memory flashbacks. That's why I had no idea what was happening to me when I started experiencing them after I left home to go to college.

I always knew that when I went away to study I wasn't going to go 'home' again. One way or another, I was going to make sure I never had to step foot in the place that had been the site of so much pain and suffering for me.

Like many victims of child abuse, I've blanked out a lot of what I went through when I was younger. My parents were both alcoholic and screaming fights were an almost nightly occurrence. It wasn't unusual for me to wake up to find blood all over the floor. It also wasn't unusual for me to be expected to clean it up or face dire punishment for not being the perfect daughter.

I know that there were times when my parents' wrath was aimed at me, but I don't remember details. Maybe there's an image of a screaming face here, or the sensation of a glass shattering against the wall next to me when it was thrown at my face, but for the most part all I know is that my childhood was not filled with sunshine and unicorns. My parents, the people I expected to protect me, were the ones I was most afraid of.

Since I don't have much in the way of visual memories, my flashbacks manifest through my body instead. It's like my body relieves the memory instead of my mind and I go through what it felt like to live the trauma.

How this feels varies depending on the trigger. The strangest of things can set them off. It could be that I'm watching a show and a mother gives a child a hug and that sets me off. I didn't even realize that was a trigger for me until it came up in one of my therapy sessions. Other times it can be sounds, like someone hitting a punching bag at the gym or a car backfiring.

When I'm experiencing a body flashback, it starts with a prickling in my palms. My heart starts to beat faster and faster. I become hypersensitive to the noises around me. The ticking of a clock can be deafening. I start feeling sick, that kind of sickness that gets you when you know you've forgotten something important but you can't remember what. It's not unlike a panic attack, which is something I also suffer from.

My therapist helped me understand that what I was going through was a body flashback which in turn helped me understand my trauma response. In some ways I'm grateful for my body flashbacks. It tells me that even though I might not remember what I went through as a child, those experiences were real and I'm not crazy. It makes it easier to be kinder to myself and understand that the damage done to me runs deep. It's going to take a long time to fully recover, if I ever will.

As I work with my therapist, I'm having fewer body memory flashbacks. I can recognize the signs of one coming on which is good. It means I can get away from people and find somewhere quiet to let it pass. It's quite distressing for other people to watch me go through a flashback and the last thing I need is to have to deal with someone else's upset while I'm trying to let the body memory pass. I focus on my breath and lean into the flashback. I've found that fighting it only makes it worse. Breathing my way through it reminds me that this will eventually pass.

I'm learning to live with my body flashbacks. It's not easy, but every day I'm grateful that I'm no longer that lost little girl living in a scary house. I'm building a brighter future and one which I refuse to let be affected by my past.

## THE IMPACT OF TRAUMA ON OUR BODIES

It's common knowledge that PTSD and Complex-PTSD causes problems for our mental health. What is less well-known is that it also harms the body.

The human brain is the greatest supercomputer ever created. Comprising around 100 billion neurons, it's constantly processing and organizing information at an unthinkingly fast rate. Between 18 and 640 trillion electric pulses are racing through your brain *every second.* Your brain is always encoding and storing your memories and experiences as we're ever growing and learning.[1]

When trauma shocks your system, it affects these memory storage processes and changes your brain. While these changes can be undone, it generally requires the support of a qualified professional1. Left unattended, they can cause emotional and physical harm for years to come. Trauma sufferers are more prone to a range of serious health conditions, including heart attack, stroke, obesity, diabetes, and cancer. What's more, the more traumatic events you've experienced, the greater the risk[2].

To all outward appearances, someone with PTSD may look perfectly fine. But the trauma will be working its insidious magic inside, lowering the body's defenses until the individual falls ill.

Why is this?

Trauma can make the brain's memory processing system malfunction so the traumatic memory isn't properly stored. Thus flashbacks are memories kept in the immediate memory store rather than the long term memory which is where they should have been placed.

Sometimes, even this is too much for the brain, so it encodes the experience as body sensations. This is a process known as dissociation, where memories are split into fragments. These fragments stay dotted about the brain, getting in the way of the brain's natural healing. This gives rise to the symptoms connected with PTSD and increases a person's chances of becoming physically sick.

There are three parts of the brain responsible for processing stress. These can change as a result of PTSD:

- The hippocampus shrinks, which is the area responsible for emotion and memory

- The amygdala function increases, which is one part of the brain controlling creativity and rumination

- The function of the prefrontal/anterior cingulate decreases, which is the area handling more complex functions such as planning and self-development.

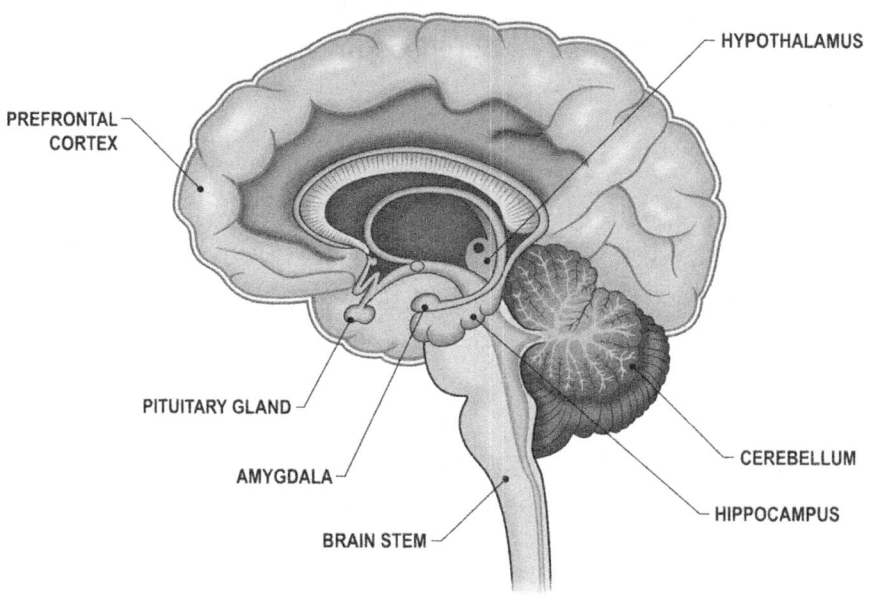

These changes can show up on brain scans[3]. However, early evidence of cellular memory suggests that this trauma doesn't just change the brain. It runs even deeper than that. It changes our body's cells too[4].

## THE IMPACT OF TRAUMA ON OUR NERVOUS SYSTEM

Trauma has been shown to affect how your body handles stress. Studies have shown that trauma affects the brain's limbic system which deals with behavioral and emotional responses. Most importantly for PTSD sufferers, it's a major player in the autonomic nervous system response we get when we're in the presence of danger - our survival instinct.

You've probably heard of the fight or flight response, but that's only half of the picture. There are two other possible responses to a threat: freeze or fawn. It used to be that one determination of whether a woman had been raped was if she fought back or said no. If not, then clearly it couldn't have been rape. She must have just regretted the sexual encounter.

Fortunately, we know better now.

It is perfectly normal to find yourself unable to fight back or scream if you are physically attacked. This is your body trying to keep you alive. This freeze or fawn response is triggered, shutting down the nervous system, dropping your metabolic rate and potentially temporarily paralyzing you.

Anyone who has been beating themselves up for not trying harder to fight off their attacker should know that their reaction was a biological, evolutionary response and nothing to do with cowardice, fear, or weakness. It's an automatic reaction, one which we can train ourselves out of, but one which none of us ever want to have to.

Trauma also affects your hypothalamic-pituitary-adrenal (HPA) axis. This is a complicated system of neuroendocrine pathways designed to keep your body in balance. Among other things, it manages stress and the stress hormone cortisol. When trauma damages the HPA axis, it can cause changes in your behavior and bodily functions, including unstable cortisol levels, major depressive disorder, anxiety, and schizophrenia.[5]

Research by the American Academy of Neurology discovered that people suffering from neurological disorders like stroke, headaches, or epilepsy were more likely to have also suffered abuse, neglect or household dysfunction when they were children.

When Larkin wrote, "They mess you up, your mum and dad. They might not mean to, but they do," he probably didn't realize just how deep that damage could run[6].

It's believed that this link probably comes down to how the neurological system develops during childhood under the influence of trauma. A traumatic event makes your body produce more adrenaline and cortisol to trigger the fight or flight response. When that trauma remains unresolved, this response can occur even if there's no actual threat - such as when you experience a flashback. This may be what causes long-term emotional and behavioral health problems[7].

## IGNORING YOUR TRAUMA

A traumatic experience isn't fun, to make the understatement of the century. It's natural to just want to try to forget about it. It's a basic human instinct to avoid pain.

I'm not going to tell you that attempting to ignore your trauma isn't a valid response. It's absolutely a choice you can make. Indeed, it's a choice *I* made for many years. 30 years of drink and drugs was my attempt to pretend I was fine.

The problem is that you can't just 'fuhgeddaboudit.' Trauma has worked its way into your brain, into your body, into your nervous system. So instead, we look to other ways of avoiding feeling all that pain, a process called trauma blocking.

This looks different for every trauma suffering, but typical behaviors include:

- Excessive use of social media, mindlessly scrolling for hours

- Binge drinking

- Mindless overeating, even if you're not hungry

- Compulsive exercising in a bid to achieve fitness goals that never satisfy you

- Doing anything to avoid being alone, even if it means staying in a toxic relationship

- Feeling uncomfortable or agitated if you have nothing to do.

- Always needing to have a project on the go

- Compulsive online shopping

- Running up debts

- Being a workaholic or having little or no boundaries at work so you're available all hours

One of the reasons why it's so hard to give up these behaviors is that when you stop using them to block your pain, that pain comes flooding back. It's overwhelming and if you haven't got a healthier mechanism in place to cope with it, it's easier to fall back into old habits. This is why it was so hard for me to stop self-medicating for so long.

The thing is that as you turn to trauma blocking behaviors, the calm peace they induce only lasts so long. The brain adjusts and so you need to increase the behavior to continue to numb the pain.

Don't get me wrong. In the moment, trauma blocking behaviors can be *great!* I went to some fantastic parties in my day, even if I can't remember them now...

Those designer clothes, round-the-world trips, expensive cars and houses you buy with the bonuses you get from working 24/7 can make you feel amazing - for a brief moment. The problem is, it doesn't last. You don't continue to feel great about the car in your driveway because it represents everything you're trying to forget. So you turn back to those behaviors that got you there, wondering why it doesn't matter how high you fly at work or how much you party, you're never happy.

While you're doing your best to block out the trauma, your body and mind are still processing what's happened. That trauma will come out whether you like it or not in the form of flashbacks, nightmares, panic attacks, triggers or intrusive thoughts as your body tries to process the trauma you're so desperate to avoid.

In trying to avoid your trauma, all you're really doing is making it worse.

Self-awareness is key to tackling trauma. Understanding that there were parts of my behavior that had a perfectly rational explanation and weren't just something I had to live with was a huge weight off my mind. It made it easier for me to start doing the work of tackling my trauma first instead of running away from it.

When you start looking into the damage trauma does to us, it gets pretty scary. And that's only the tip of the iceberg. In the next chapter, we're going to look at the bigger picture of trauma and how it's been affecting your life in ways you probably didn't even know about.

*Pause here and spend a few minutes with your Workbook that has a helpful reflection exercise for you*

# HOW TRAUMA TRIES TO RUN OUR LIFE

**Trauma Is More Than Just Bad Memories. It's The Gift You Don't Want That Just Keeps Giving.**

*Days when you only feel 30%, an effort of 30% is 100% of your ability. Some days you'll want to run 20 kms, some days getting to the shower and brushing your teeth seems like climbing Everest. Wake up, get vertical, listen to your body and do your best.*

## DON'S STORY:

When I was first posted to Iraq, I was filled with conflicting emotions. I was excited about doing some good in the world, but I was also nervous about what was going to happen. This was my first active duty.

I remember I'd been in Iraq for only a few hours, still at the airport. A bunch of us were lying on the gravel by the runway, the only available place where we might be able to get some sleep. We'd been traveling for days, all sick from a combination of antibiotics, vaccines, awful army food and nerves. Those moments lying with my friends were weirdly relaxing, but it was the last time I'd feel that kind of peace.

It wasn't long before someone came and passed out loaded magazines. Then someone else came with grenades. It was one thing after another until we all had our full range of kit. That was the moment when I felt like a real soldier. This wasn't a drill. This was real life with real ammo and a real chance of death.

Most of the time, active duty's boring. There's not a lot to do and Iraq is hot, arid and dusty. The women won't even look you in the eye because they're afraid they'll be punished by the men in their family.

But when you see action ...

There are some things I'll never forget. I can't even talk about them without choking up. One of my closest army friends was blown-up by a land-mine just a few feet away from me. I was haunted by the sensation of his body raining down around me and plagued by guilt that he was the one who died and not me.

I haven't been able to shake those memories, even though I've been out of the army for years. I got a job in a call center and there would be times when the sound of a phone ringing would put me right back on the battlefield. The smell of gas when I was filling up my car would remind me of driving while under fire.

My then-girlfriend encouraged me to socialize with other ex-military men, but I soon discovered all it did was make me remember the bad times. That was the last thing I wanted. Yet there were other things I couldn't remember. My mind seemed to be playing tricks on me.

My relationship didn't survive long after I got back. I'd been so looking forward to seeing my girlfriend again. She'd booked us a nice hotel room for my first night home, ordered in my favorite foods and a large crate of beer. But I couldn't relax. The sound of a door slamming down the corridor would make me jump and look for my gun.

It wasn't much better at home. I struggled to fall asleep and then I'd wake up early. I was subsisting off a few hours' sleep a night. I was irritable and my poor girlfriend always got the worst of my moods.

I started drinking heavily to try and dull the pain. A few drinks would make me aggressive and I'd go looking for a fight. It was too much for my girlfriend to take so she left.

It took me a while, but I've managed to cut back on my drinking although I'm not completely sober. I did go for therapy for a while, but I found talking about my past made things worse. Right now, I'm taking things one step at a time while I figure out how I'm supposed to live with the mess that's in my brain. I'm doing yoga and that helps. Maybe one day I'll go back to therapy, but I'm not ready yet.

## THE RELATIONSHIP BETWEEN TRAUMA AND PTSD

Most of us will experience at least one traumatic event in our lives. This could be the unexpected loss of a loved one, being attacked, being in a serious accident, or suffering a life-threatening illness or injury. All of these things are horrific for the person going through it, yet the rate of PTSD remains relatively low. Not everyone suffering a traumatic event will develop mental health problems[1].

So what causes some people to develop PTSD and others to continue with their lives unscathed?

The short answer is, we don't yet fully know. It is believed that it's due to a range of influences, including biological, psychological, social, demographical, historical, and political factors. What we *do* know is that certain things place you at a greater risk of developing PTSD (although it's not guaranteed):

- Age. Generally speaking, the younger you are when you experience trauma, the greater the effect.

- Gender. Women are more likely to develop PTSD than men.

- Low levels of education.

- Low levels of social support.

- Living in areas with a history of war or colonization.

- Suffering sexual violence.

- Pre-existing mental health issues.

- Adverse childhood experiences.

The WHO (World Health Organization) carried out a series of surveys into mental health, including trauma-specific PTSD, which threw up some interesting findings that may go some way to explaining why two people going through the same trauma could result in one developing PTSD and not the other:

- Someone with a history of trauma, particularly physical violence, had a much greater risk of PTSD when going through subsequent traumas.

- Losing a loved one unexpectedly is a common form of trauma but carries a relatively low risk of PTSD.

- In comparison, sexual violence or violence from a partner had the highest risk of PTSD.

- The average length of PTSD symptoms was 72.3 months, or around six years.

- Those traumatized by combat had the most persistent symptoms.

- Meanwhile, those who'd gone through a natural disaster had the least persistent symptoms[2].

The problem is that PTSD is hard to research due to its nature. Many PTSD surveys need participants to describe their experiences which isn't always reliable. For years, I simply wouldn't talk about what I went through. I didn't want anyone to think I was less of a man. The male need to appear strong may be an explanation for why women are statistically more likely to develop PTSD - men may be less likely to seek help or describe the true extent of what they're going through. *Guys! We need to talk*

I've noticed I'm not alone in this. As I've started working with others with PTSD, I've found that many of us find it hard to talk about our trauma and its impact on our lives. This means that trauma could be far more prevalent than the statistics would have us believe, something I'm personally inclined to agree with.

## THE DIFFERENCE BETWEEN PTSD AND COMPLEX PTSD

We now think that the condition called 'shell shock' back in World War I was actually PTSD. Complex-PTSD as a distinct definition is in fact relatively new, only recognized in the 1980s. The WHO's International Classification of Diseases (ICD-11) published in 2018 included Complex PTSD (C-PTSD) as a disorder in its own right for the first time, joining PTSD as a 'Disorder specifically associated with stress.'

However, at the time of writing, C-PTSD is not recognized as a separate condition in the *Diagnostic and Statistical Manual of Mental Disorders, 5th edition (DSM-5)*, the definitive handbook used by psychiatrists and psychologists in the USA and around the world to define mental health disorders. Sadly, not all therapists are aware of C-PTSD, so it can be hard to get a diagnosis.

C-PTSD covers more complex reactions that arise in people who've had to deal with chronic trauma. Both PTSD and C-PTSD are complicated conditions which share many symptoms. Since the treatments for both tend to be similar and overlap, the information in this book is aimed at people suffering from both PTSD and C-PTSD. However, it should be born in mind that there are some differences between the two:

- PTSD usually arises following a single trauma, such as difficult childbirth, an assault, or an accident.

- C-PTSD develops as a result of sustained or repeated traumatic events, such as bullying, chronic abuse or violence, emergency service workers handling life-or-death situations, victims of slavery or human trafficking, prisoners of war, or prisoners held in solitary confinement for sustained periods. It is more common among those who went through trauma during an earlier stage of development or were abused by someone who should have been trustworthy, such as a parent or guardian.

These aren't hard and fast rules though. You can get C-PTSD after an isolated traumatic incident, just as you can get PTSD following multiple traumas.

The symptoms are similar for PTSD and C-PTSD:

- Reliving the trauma through flashbacks, intrusive thoughts, and nightmares

- Avoiding triggers that are reminiscent of the trauma

- Changes in mood and thoughts, including feeling detached from others or feeling overwhelmingly negative

- Hyperalertness, feeling irritable, or easily frightened/ startled

- Problems with concentration

- Insomnia

C-PTSD also brings with it some extra symptoms:

- Problems regulating emotions. This could result in an explosive temper, ongoing sadness or depression or suicidal ideation. Sufferers may feel detached from reality or struggle to feel happy.

- Fixating on the abuser or wanting to get revenge on them.

- Negative self-image. Someone with C-PTSD may feel helpless, guilty, or ashamed. They may also feel like they are unlike other people.

- Problems with relationships. Sufferers may find it hard to trust others. Their negative self-view may make it difficult to bond with others in a healthy way. Someone with C-PTSD may fall into toxic relationships because they don't know any different or they may avoid relationships altogether.

- A sense of hopelessness about the future.

- Detachment from the trauma. Sufferers can disconnect from themselves or the world around them. It's even possible that they may forget their trauma. I know that I'll never remember everything I went through growing up.

- Losing a sense of religion, belief, value, or trust.

- Problems with self-esteem. C-PTSD sufferers can erroneously blame themselves for what they went through, somehow thinking that what happened was because of some fault in themselves.

## ANXIETY AND TRAUMA

Back when I was at my worst, I'd often feel irrationally anxious. I'd worry about whether my boss liked my work. I'd worry about what was going to happen at a party. I'd have panic attacks before gigs. There were times when I had to practically force myself to go to a club, even though I knew it was essential for my career, which I took a great deal of pride in.

Turns out trauma and anxiety often go hand in hand. Dealing with one is bad enough. Dealing with *both* can be exhausting, debilitating and incredibly frustrating. It just isn't fair. Why should we be the ones to have to cope with all this on top of everything we've been through?

*If you've felt this, you're not alone*

Ever tried to answer the question of which came first - the chicken or the egg? So it is with trauma and anxiety. If you already suffer from anxiety, it's possible you're more likely to develop PTSD. At the same time, a traumatic situation could trigger anxiety. You might have been fine going into crowded places, but find yourself having panic attacks at the very thought following a traumatic event. That panic attack could make you feel like you were going to die, but if nobody notices, you're on your own. That can be a further source of trauma. This then triggers a downward spiral where you become terrified of future panic attacks, which could bring on panic disorder.

While treating anxiety might relieve your PTSD and vice versa, it could also make things worse because you're leaving a serious set of symptoms unaddressed. So, when you're looking to heal your PTSD using the methods outlined later in this book, make sure you pay attention to your anxiety as well. Caring for yourself on a holistic level is the only way you're going to see long lasting, genuine results. *Please remember this*

## ATTACHMENT DISORDERS AND TRAUMA

Do you bounce from one toxic relationship to another? Feel like you'll never find the right man or woman for you? Think you don't deserve love?

Feel like there's something wrong with you? I certainly did. I felt unlovable, unsafe in my own skin and like a fraud a lot of the time.

I want to tell you there's nothing wrong with you. We all deserve  love. But if you had a difficult relationship with your primary caregiver when you were a child, you may have developed attachment trauma. Its effects can last long after your childhood has passed - in some cases for whole lifetimes.

As the Jesuits say, give me a man until he's seven and I will show you the man. Our early childhood experiences shape the patterns of our adult life. Our relationship with our primary caregiver is one of the most important in determining whether we enjoy healthy relationships as an adult - or not.

We turn to our caregivers to meet all our needs. These range from the basics - food and shelter - to affection, support and emotional stability. If these needs aren't met, this can leave children alone while they somehow have to find ways of coping with highly charged emotional states.

When your caregiver gives you stress rather than care, this can result in attachment trauma. It can also lead to C-PTSD if you suffer chronic abuse or neglect. While 'attachment parenting' is a major buzzword at the moment, we don't talk so much about the flip side of the coin. While we're increasingly aware of the importance of meeting a child's needs when raising healthy individuals, we don't talk as much about what happens in their absence.

We mentioned body flashbacks earlier in this book and attachment trauma can cause this. The very idea of a relationship can send your nervous system into fight, flight, freeze, or flood mode. Your nervous system is always learning how to connect with those around you, particularly when you're a child and your body is developing. Your childhood experiences may have taught you that it's simply not safe to be in connection with other people.

So, if you've been wondering why the idea of being with someone is such a source of stress for you, you may have just found the answer. You may also be a magnet for further abuse. Not having had positive relationships modeled for you as a child, you may have no idea about what this should look like. So, you attract toxic individuals because it's hard for you to realize that there *are* alternatives.

You might go in the opposite direction. Rather than being afraid of intimacy, you're afraid of being alone, so you end up in codependent relationships or stay with someone long after a relationship has hit its use-by date because the thought of being single is simply terrifying.

By now you may be feeling overwhelmed. When you realize just how insidious trauma is and just how deeply it's got its claws into your life, it can be unsettling to say the least. But there's a reason why I've given you all this information. Self-awareness is one of the most powerful weapons you have in the fight against PTSD.

In the next chapter we're going to start digging into your personal trauma experiences. We'll look at triggers, what they are, and what to do when you're triggered.

*Spend a moment with your Workbook to reflect*

# THE EFFECTS
# OF TRAUMA

How Trauma Shows Up In Your Daily Life
And What You Can Do About It

*When all you know is fight or flight, red flags and
butterflies all feel the same.*

*– Cindy Cherie*

## ALICE'S STORY:

I remember waking up one morning and feeling disappointed that I hadn't died in my sleep. It was a Saturday and I didn't have to go anywhere which was good because I was physically incapable of getting out of bed. I only managed to drag myself out a few hours later because of a need to use the bathroom, but afterwards I crawled right back into bed again. I couldn't see anything positive about my life. I had a job, colleagues who respected me, but none of it mattered. I was crushed by an overwhelming sense of dread without any idea of what I was dreading.

It wasn't the first time I felt like this. I didn't want to go on if this was what life was going to be like. Seven years later, I'm out of that deep, dark tunnel and living in the light - but it was a real journey to get here.

My dad left when I was nine. I felt relieved at the time. He'd been psychologically abusive towards me and my mother. I was always on edge, not knowing what tiny transgression would set him off.

There was one time when I came inside after building a snowman. I was freezing and my mom made me a mug of hot cocoa. At the time, there were adverts for soup in a mug that showed people lacing their fingers through the mug handle to wrap their hand around the mug to warm it. I copied them, thinking it would be a nice way to make my hands warmer after playing in the snow.

Instantly, my dad snapped, yelling at me about how that wasn't how you used a mug, that the handle was there for a reason, and how could he have a daughter so stupid to not understand that? I've never been able to drink from a mug since.

It was so nice after he left not to have to worry about whether I was eating my food properly or tying my shoelaces the right way. But when my parents officially divorced, the court ordered that I spend weekends and vacations with him.

Living with just my mom had been fun. She was sweet and kind and funny. But knowing that I had to see my dad at the weekend put me on edge all week. I stressed about what might happen when I went to stay with him. It was a different time back then. There wasn't the support for children who were being bullied by their parents. Anyway, I didn't talk about it. Who was going to believe me? I was just a kid.

When I was about 13, I developed anxiety. I was constantly terrified, which made me exhausted all the time. It was almost impossible to do my best at school, which of course gave my dad another excuse to yell at me. I didn't have any real friends either. Looking back, I can see how I put up walls between me and other people. They were there to protect me from my dad but they also cut me off from any possible help.

Things hit rock bottom just after I graduated college. I'd rented my first apartment and that summer it was broken into. It was very traumatic and although I thought I was okay about it, I now know that all I'd done was hidden my emotions. Later that year my Meemaw (grandmother) died suddenly. She was one of the few bright lights of my childhood and it felt like part of my life died with her.

After that it was soon obvious I was far from okay. I became obsessive, checking I'd locked the door multiple times before I could leave then looking outside my apartment building to make sure there weren't any possible threats. It got harder and harder to leave the house. I was crying every day.

Finally, my boss took me to one side and told me he'd noticed my work wasn't as good as it used to be. He suggested I go see a therapist and that's when I was diagnosed with C-PTSD along with anxiety disorder.

I started treatment for my PTSD and slowly things began to improve. I had no idea so much of my behavior had been caused by trauma. I used to comfort shop and was heavily in debt as a consequence. Now I understand the urge to shop was caused by my mental health and I'm slowly getting my debt under control.

It's taken me a while, but I finally feel like I'm becoming the person I was born to be. My past doesn't have to shape my future. I'm taking back control of my life one day at a time.

## LIVING WITH TRAUMA

Trauma is rapacious. It burrows into all aspects of your life. If you experienced trauma as a child, you may be unaware of how much it's shaped who you are. You may well be living with the symptoms and think that it's just who you are without knowing that it's a trauma response and something you probably won't have to live with once you've tackled the root cause.

Night terrors. Irritability. Insomnia. Lack of focus. Mood swings. Self-harm. Alcohol or drug abuse. All of these are symptoms of trauma - and that's not all of them. When you find yourself doing or saying things and not knowing why, or you head down self-destructive paths knowing full well it's not where you want to go, that's your trauma taking charge. I struggled with this for so long. I've always had a really strong work ethic, could apply myself to a range of situations and work models, but there was always this "Jekyyl and Hyde" creature lurking in the shadows, ready to drive me to self sabotage at the drop of a hat.

Trauma manifests differently in everyone. How I responded to my trauma might not be how you react to yours. Some people are able to successfully mask it, keeping their struggles to themselves until they become too much to bear. This is why it's so important to talk about your trauma with someone, even if you think you're coping. Trauma can rear its ugly head days, months, or even years after the initial event.  *Please do this.*

## THE EMOTIONAL SIGNS OF TRAUMA

Trauma affects us on a holistic level. No part of your being is safe from its devastation.

One of the most common ways trauma comes out is through your emotions. You may find yourself feeling denial, anger, or sadness without any obvious reason. Or you might find yourself overreacting to a book or movie, sobbing your eyes out over a cute little puppy or the sight of a happy family without being able to explain why - because you don't know.

You may suffer from emotional outbursts. Often, victims of trauma retarget their strong emotions towards others as a coping mechanism. It may lighten the load in the moment, but it means your friends and loved ones end up suffering alongside you.

Trauma can push the very people away who might have been able to help you through it. It takes a very understanding partner to stay with someone hell bent on self-destruction because their trauma is just too much.

You could suffer from intrusive thoughts, nightmares, flashbacks, forcing you to relieve the trauma, either in whole or with little snippets. Music was one of my triggers. Sounds, smells might take you back to a moment you were abused. A place might remind you of the accident you were in. As a result you start avoiding people or places that remind you of your trauma. You step back from social events or activities that used to bring you so much joy.

You may develop anxiety or panic attacks, obsessions and compulsions. You might feel emotionally numb or detached or you could feel depression, shame, and even guilt, especially if you survived a traumatic event while others didn't.

Persistent negative feelings, however they present, are a possible sign of trauma[1].

## THE PHYSICAL SIGNS OF TRAUMA

While we may think trauma is 'only' in the mind, it has very real physical effects as well as Bessel van der Kolk wrote, in The Body Keeps The Score. It remembers everything we've been through, good and bad. Pent up trauma can manifest in physical symptoms, including lethargy and fatigue. If you've been feeling chronically tired for years, struggling to find the motivation to do anything much beyond binge watching *The Tiger King* for the umpteenth time, it could be down to your body attempting to protect you from trauma.

But the physical symptoms of trauma may run even deeper. The gut is sometimes known as the second brain because of the impact it has on brain function and the rest of the body. Indeed, there are approximately 100 billion neurons in the human brain (the cells that tell your body how to behave) but the gut has 500 million neurons connected to the brain via the nervous system[2]. It is now recognized that there is a connection between trauma and gut health.

For example, trauma survivors are more likely to develop irritable bowel syndrome (IBS), which brings with it a range of symptoms, including stomach ache, diarrhea, bloating, constipation, gas, and cramps. Those bathroom problems you thought were simply one of those things? Your old friend trauma.

Trauma also lowers the immune system by affecting the 'good' bacteria living in your gut. These have a crucial role in controlling the immune system. While we don't yet know whether there is a definite connection between trauma, the immune system and gut inflammation, it is true that people with PTSD frequently have problems with their immune system. And when your immune system is compromised, it's harder for your body to fight off disease and infections.

Your gut microbiome also impacts other systems in the body, such as your endocrine system, your central nervous system and your metabolism. These systems are all essential to survival, so when trauma prevents their smooth functioning, your body can barely look after itself let alone support you through the healing you so desperately need.

Research has also shown that gut health plays a major role in depression. When your gut flora is imbalanced, you can develop depression. If you were traumatized as a child, this depression can interfere with your brain's development, impacting your ability to deal with stress when you're an adult. If you had a parent who told you what a failure you were as a child, they were actively setting you up for failure later in life - it's literally been programmed into your gut.

## TRAUMA TRIGGERS

 *"I feel so triggered."*

The word "triggered" has been tossed about so much in recent years that it's almost become a joke. Yet if you've genuinely been triggered by something you'll know it's nothing to laugh about. I know when mine would kick in, I would feel tension in my chest, like I was having a heart attack.

A trigger is anything that causes you to relive a traumatic experience. Obvious triggers could be detailed descriptions or depictions of a traumatic event, but they can also be subtle like songs, smells, or colors. Someone suffering from PTSD due to medical trauma might find it hard to watch hospital dramas. A traumatic birth could make it difficult to watch scenes of someone giving birth, even if the film or show is light hearted.

Let's say it's your birthday party. You've just blown out the candles on your cake and you've cut into the cake. That delicious, chocolatey aroma hits your nose and your mouth starts to water in anticipation of that sweet cake.

You put a forkful of cake in your mouth, closing your eyes to savor the taste. At that moment, you hear a thud. There's a scream and you open your eyes to see your father collapsed on the floor suffering a massive heart attack. Instinctively you throw up the cake.

After that day, you always feel a little weird around your birthday, like you're disconnected from your emotions. You don't like going to birthday parties because you find them upsetting. Just the thought of chocolate cake makes you want to vomit. The smell of chocolate brings back the sound of that terrifying thud.

Triggers can place you right back in the time of your trauma and cause a physical or emotional reaction such as panic attacks, crying, anger, or sadness. This is why trigger warnings are becoming increasingly popular so those with PTSD can make an informed choice over whether they want to put themselves at risk of being triggered.

While trigger warnings can be helpful in letting you know that content might be problematic, the problem is that different people have different triggers. Some triggers can be obscure and unpredictable. You may have been attacked and be fine about watching violent movies yet struggle to breath if the song that was playing at the time comes on the radio.

Trigger warnings may also create a false impression of trauma sufferers as being overly sensitive or in need of constant protection. Conversely, they can also result in people thinking that someone claiming they've been triggered is being over-sensitive. And unfortunately, given the overuse of the phrase, when faced with material someone finds offensive, the true effect of a trigger is diminished.

It's even possible that trigger warnings can be harmful to those who haven't been traumatized. One study found that people with no history of trauma nevertheless felt more vulnerable and anxious when presented with a trigger warning before reading potentially upsetting content[3].

If you have triggers for your trauma, it can be difficult to talk about it. Maybe you've had people dismiss your experience or you worry about sounding stupid. However, you don't deserve to be triggered. And you certainly shouldn't be putting your own needs below anyone else's.

If someone brings up a trigger for you, here's some suggestions on how to deal with it:

- **Be specific.** Tell them exactly how you felt and why. "When you said *xyz,* it made me feel stressed and nervous because of past experiences."

- **Give them a boundary.** Let them know what you can deal with and what will happen if they ignore your boundaries. "It's difficult for me to discuss *xyz.* If you want to talk about it, I'll need to leave."

- **Ask for a warning in future.** "I know it can be hard to avoid talking about xyz. Could you please warn me if it's likely to come up in discussion?"

Remember that your experience is your experience and it's completely valid. Not everyone who's been through a traumatic event will develop triggers. Two people could go through the same trauma but have very different responses. Understanding your personal triggers and not making comparisons to anyone else will help you develop coping strategies until you're able to get treatment to deal with your trauma and its triggers.

We've covered some pretty heavy material in the first part of this book. It's been designed to give you a stronger understanding of just how deep the damage lies so you can start untangling what's trauma and what's you.

So, when you're ready, let's move on to the things you can do to finally start the recovery from your trauma.

# PART 2

## Process

It's one thing to know what you 'should' do. It's another thing altogether to know how to do it.

In this next part, we're going to examine what your journey to recovery may look like and what sort of experiences may come up for you along the way. When you know what's normal and what you can expect, it increases the chances of sticking with the process when you encounter challenges.

There will be times when you feel like you're regressing, but I promise, your willingness to confront your trauma and take steps to heal means that you're making enormous progress. It will be hard at times. You'll want to quit regularly. I know I did. The comfort of what you know will feel safer than the unknown territory you're stepping into. That's your ego trying to protect you. But, again, I promise, your healing will lead you to a place that will make all the challenges worthwhile.

I'm here for you.

Keep going.

# HEALING
# IS TOUGH

## What To Expect Along This Path

*This process isn't linear. You'll have good days and bad days. Make the most of the good days and make peace with the bad days.*

## CAITLIN'S STORY:

The first time I saw my therapist, I said, "I don't think I'll ever be able to recover from what I went through. I've tried so many things, but I just can't get past it, no matter how much I want to."

I'll never forget her response: "If healing from trauma were easy, no one would have any issues."

I don't remember when the abuse began. I can't. I was too young. All I know is that it started when my mom's brother moved in some time after my first birthday and it stopped when he died from a stroke when I was eight.

My childhood was characterized by danger. I wasn't safe at home. I was frequently left alone with my uncle and I thought what he was doing to me was normal. Of course I did. I'd never known any different.

It took me almost thirty years to start getting help and then it was only because of a throwaway remark from a colleague when they read about a high profile child abuse case. She said, "I don't know how that child's ever going to lead a normal life. They're going to need a ton of therapy."

I hadn't been following along with the story. I couldn't. It brought back too many difficult memories and emotions. But in that moment I felt an overwhelming sense of grief. Grief for the innocent child I'd never been allowed to be. Grief for the life I could have had if I hadn't always felt like I didn't deserve better. I hadn't gone to college. That wasn't for people like me.

I knew something had to change, but I wasn't brave enough to go to a therapist. Not yet. Instead, I turned to the internet and read up on different ways to heal from childhood trauma. I started going to yoga classes and practicing meditation.

I discovered an inner calm I'd never felt. Finally I felt brave enough to share some of what I'd been through with people I thought I could trust. Some people were supportive, but others...

When I tried to talk about it with my family, I guess it was too hard for them to hear. I got comments like, "Your uncle isn't here to defend himself. You shouldn't talk about him like that." "It'll destroy the family if this gets out." "You should have told him to stop." "You're making it up. There's no way anything like that happened. False memories are a thing you know."

I lost friends over it. Some members of my family refuse to speak to me, even now, unless I admit to lying. Of course, I won't do that because although I might not remember every single detail, I know it happened.

About eighteen months after I started talking about what I'd been through I had my first flashback. I remember feeling like I was drowning, as if I'd never be able to breathe because my throat was closed up. I felt so deep in despair, I called a suicide hotline to help me get through.

They supported me to find a local support group for adult survivors of childhood abuse. Walking into that room was possibly the bravest thing I've ever done. When it was my turn to share my story, I felt so small, like I was a young child again, at the mercy of the adults around me.

But as I began to speak and listen to the stories of the people around me, I felt a sense of connection I'd never experienced before. I had no idea how isolated I'd felt. How ironic that I was finally finding a family among this group of strangers.

Talking over coffee after the group was finished, one of the other members gave me the card of a therapist who'd helped her. I called to make an appointment the next day before I lost my nerve. I wasn't sure it could make any difference. I'd been so lost for so long. But gradually, my therapist helped me take down the walls I'd put up to protect myself. She helped me put the abuse I'd been through in the past where it belonged.

It wasn't an easy journey to recovery. As well as going to my therapist, I devoured books, was an active member on trauma forums and went on healing retreats. There were times I felt like I was being crushed by the weight of my trauma, but I wasn't alone anymore. I had people I could call when it was all too much.

I studied trauma and its effects and was stunned by how many symptoms I was experiencing I had no idea weren't normal. The inexplicable emotional flashbacks, the hyperarousal [when the body goes into high alert as a consequence of trauma], the tears when I heard certain songs, the problems with building healthy relationships with people, instead bouncing from one toxic individual to another because I didn't feel I deserved better. Trauma had been my constant companion for practically my whole life. It was hard learning new ways of being.

I'm still seeing my therapist, but it won't be long before I won't need to anymore. I'm even planning on going to college. I'm rebuilding my life from the ground up, one brick at a time. At last,

I'm discovering what it's like to live out of the shadow of trauma and it feels amazing.

## WHY HEALING FROM TRAUMA IS SO HARD

I want to make something very clear before we go any further. The reason you haven't healed from your trauma is not because there's something wrong with you. You're not stupid. You don't love playing the victim. You're not mentally ill. You're not lazy. You're not weak. Quite the opposite. The fact you're still here is a testimony to how strong you are.

Trauma is *designed* to be hard to heal. Trauma is your brain and body's way of getting through an experience or environment in which your life was under threat or you felt powerless. If that situation wasn't taken seriously, there's a very real possibility you wouldn't survive. You are meant to have an extreme reaction to extreme situations. You're meant to try and avoid putting yourself in a position where it could happen again. All the symptoms of trauma are simply your brain and body's attempts to keep you safe in the future. It's well-meaning and well-intentioned.

As far as your body and brain is concerned, it's better to be alive and traumatized than dead. Unfortunately, the things you need to recover from your trauma are the things your trauma pushes away. It's a Catch-22 but it's not one you willingly signed up for.

There are a number of ways in which trauma makes it hard for you to heal. Firstly, it shuts down the front part of the brain. The part that plays a crucial role in healing.

A very simplified view of the brain (and one that you don't need to be a neuroscientist to understand) is to think of the brain as being in two halves. The back brain deals with all the unconscious automated functions, like breathing, your heart beating, and reflexes.

The front brain is the conscious mind. It's the part that thinks, reflects, plans and rationalizes our experiences. In a traumatic situation, this part of the brain switches off, so our automatic responses ruled by the back brain can take over. This part of the brain doesn't care about your feelings or emotions. It drives us towards what it thinks are safe behaviors and gives us a negative view of the world. We assume that the worst will happen in future so our traumatized state keeps us at a high state of alert to effectively deal with it.

As we heal from our trauma, we need to nurture the front brain so it can take back control of our processes. We need to make conscious choices over knee jerk reactions; assess potential risks rationally rather than jumping to worst case scenarios; deal with new situations on their own merits rather than relying on old patterns of behavior. We need our front brain to formulate a recovery plan and help us navigate any obstacles like poverty, unemployment, relationship problems, and lack of access to treatment while keeping the back brain firmly in its place.

So, for example, if you feel ready to go to therapy but can't afford it, you need your front brain firing on all cylinders so it can formulate a plan. It needs to identify all potential options, even if they're seemingly impossible, take action and not be deterred by setbacks, find the right support, assess prospective therapists to find the right one and actually show up to appointments. Do not underestimate how challenging this all is. It requires a functioning front brain to be able to cope with it.

If your back brain is running the show, it'll slide into its default state of 'I can't.' You'll give up before you even try because it's been programmed by trauma to enter a state of freeze. In trauma, trying to fight back is pointless and that same state of helplessness is brought forward into other situations.

The front brain is the part that imagines a life free of trauma and draws up a list of options for how we can make that happen. The back brain has a fixed, black-and-white mindset that 'knows' that nothing will ever change so there's no point in trying something different. The front brain could find a way through the mess, but the back brain is putting the brakes on. It's only trying to protect you, keep you safe from disappointment or hurt, not to mention ensuring you never get traumatized again. Safety is the primary concern of the back brain. Nothing else matters, including your mental health.

It is very difficult to break out of this programming. Trauma puts the back brain in charge and keeps it there. The one tool we have that can get us out of this state - the front brain - is switched off by trauma. It's a cycle that's almost impossible to break free from.

Trauma also installs in us a fear of people, but our neurobiology requires people for us to feel safe. It's another paradoxical thing our brains and bodies do with the very best of intentions that causes more harm in the long run.

There is a research protocol dubbed 'The Strange Situation' that explores the importance of attachment to caregivers. A scenario was set up in which a one-year-old is allowed to play in a room with their primary caregiver. The caregiver leaves the room a couple of times while the child plays, leaving the child alone on one occasion and on another with a stranger. The child's reactions were observed not just to being separated from their caregiver but also to being reunited with them.

One of the most intriguing findings was that when the child did not have a strong connection with their caregiver, they were unsure what to do when they returned to the room. Would it be safe to go to the caregiver for comfort or was it better to avoid them so they wouldn't get into trouble?

Some children had very dramatic reactions to this situation. Some fell to the ground and didn't move, shut down in a dissociative state. Others moved towards their caregiver, but backwards, a curious mix of approach and avoid. This state has been termed 'disorganized attachment' because there's no effective way to feel safe with someone who makes you feel unsafe. It's a fear with no satisfactory resolution[1].

This is how trauma works in adults. When our trauma has been caused by the actions of other people, we're stuck. We need people to help heal us, but our problems have been caused by people. Our back brains, only concerned with our safety, warn us to keep our distance and don't show any vulnerability. So, when we sit in close proximity with a therapist to explore our deepest, darkest places, this provokes fear of what we need the most. We stress about sharing what we've been through with our therapist because they could use it against us. This paradox needs the front brain to be brave to push through and expose those places to the light so they can heal. But our natural reaction is to hide away.

Finally, we need effective tools to tackle our distress but we weren't ever given them in childhood. Trauma by its very nature is distressing. We may not always feel it, especially if we were young at the time of our exposure to trauma, but on some level, our brains and bodies are desperate to escape. That distress is necessary because it pushes us to do something to change the situation. Even if you don't consciously feel distressed, that emotion expresses itself in other ways, such as dysregulation. This is when we feel emotionally and physically upset and can't settle down. We know we need to feel differently but we just can't find that inner sense of calm and safety.

From the moment we're born, we learn to regulate our emotions from other people: our parents, guardians and other caregivers. We're soothed by physical touch, eye contact, gentle movements, quiet reassurances that no matter what's happening, everything's going to be alright.

If an adult is going to be able to regulate a child, they need to be regulated themselves. You can't calm someone else if you're not calm yourself. This is how trauma becomes generational. A traumatized parent can't regulate themselves so can't regulate their child, no matter how much they may want to. Thus a consistently dysregulated parent can be very frightening for the child, putting them at risk of trauma.

When a caregiver can soothe a baby, the infant's brain builds neural networks to transport calming chemicals around the brain. But if you're exposed to frequent trauma, no matter how supportive the caregiver, that terror and threat interferes with the building of this network. So when the child matures into adulthood, instead of having a brain with a solid infrastructure, there are all sorts of miswirings and missing connections. It's still possible to self-soothe, but sometimes it's a major effort and can take the brain a while to find alternative ways through. This is why some, like myself, turn to alcohol or drugs to numb the pain. They simply physically can't do it themselves.

When you decide you're ready to recover from trauma, you need others to hold space for you, be a safe, soothing presence while you process your experiences. But some trauma survivors are often alone during times of distress without basic social support and the thought of turning to someone for help is scary because of how people have treated us in the past. The calming chemicals the brain can release to soothe us get lost and don't go to where they need to go.

This is the worst paradox of trauma: if we weren't so traumatized, we'd be in a much better position to recover from trauma. You can't just suddenly 'get over it.' Trauma only cares that you survive. It's not bothered if you thrive. Once you understand that, it becomes easier to forgive yourself for finding this so tough - because it *is* tough.

## WHY CHANGE IS SO DIFFICULT

Humans are creatures of habit. One of the biggest challenges we face is making long-term, sustained changes that we know are in our best interests. Whether you want to change your diet, establish exercise routines, break free of addictions - or heal your trauma - changing your behavior is one of the hardest things you'll ever do. Research has shown that there's a number of reasons for this.

We're more motivated by negative emotions than positive. While you'd think that the guilt, shame, and fear that come from your trauma would be a big enough trigger for you to break free, they have the opposite effect. Negative emotions can make us think about all the things we're not doing, or make us criticize ourselves because we're not doing things the 'right' way. In fact, one review of over a hundred behavior change studies found that fear and regret were the least effective drivers for change. If you want to heal from trauma, you'll need positive reasons for moving on[2].

This negativity can tie us up in a black-and-white view of our trauma. You think that you're going to try to heal your trauma, but if you don't do it quickly or you have a setback, that must mean you aren't capable of ever being well. This all-or-nothing thinking sets you up for failure because trauma recovery isn't a linear process. You'll have good days and bad days. The bad days don't mean you're not getting better. They're just bad days. But they can be enough to make you stop trying[3].

We neglect to give ourselves the tools we need to see the process through. If you were fixing a leaky sink, you'd make sure you had all the tools you needed before starting. Why should fixing your mind be any different? You need a number of reliable mechanisms to support these changes you're making. You'll find plenty later in this book so you can tailor your recovery program to suit your preferences.

We underestimate just how long it's going to take. Change is never a one-and-done process. It's probably taken you years to reach the point where you're able to pick up this book and think about doing the hard work. Why would you then think you're going to have an overnight miracle?

Sustained recovery can't happen without a process that takes into account everything you're dealing with. Long-term change requires steps, usually little ones. I know we all wish that trauma was easy to recover from, but by its very nature, it's incredibly hard. You need to focus on the future you're trying to build and understand that consistent effort is required to get there. It takes as long as it takes.

Remember, you're going to fall and stumble along the way. It's inevitable that there will be moments when you'll want to give up. You'll need to face your trauma head-on, which can involve reliving the worst times of your life. You might find that there are days when you don't want to get out of bed. It might get worse before it gets better. Your back brain will fight the process because it's still focused on safety and doesn't care about happiness. Happiness is a luxury and one we can live without.

Lasting recovery includes accepting that these 'failures' are all part of the process and are, in fact, signs of your progress. They signal how far you've come and your dedication to the process should be celebrated.

Since it's crucial to be prepared for your worst days so you can push through to the other side, we're going to take the next chapter to explore the two biggest self-saboteurs you're going to encounter: your mind and your anxious thoughts.

# IMAGINARY
# THREATS
# AND TRIGGERS

## How Your Own Mind Can Get
## In The Way Of Your Recovery

*Healing trauma involves tears.*
*The tears release our pain.*
*The tears are part of our recovery.*
*My friend, please let your tears flow.*

*– Dana Arcuri*

## ELLIE'S STORY:

They say I'll never remember exactly what happened when I was involved in a major car accident. I suppose I should be grateful for that. I still can't bring myself to watch the dashcam footage that recorded what happened.

Apparently, the front wheel of my car caught a pothole at exactly the wrong angle. The tire burst and my car went careening across the road, hitting another oncoming car at a combined speed of over 110mph.

I still have flashbacks where I'm coming to in my car, the smell of smoke tickling my nostrils. Instinctively, I knew I needed to get out. I didn't want to be burned alive in my car.

I ached all over, but somehow I managed to pull myself out of my car and drag myself along the road to a safe distance. I passed out again and next thing I knew I was in an ambulance.

The next few hours are a haze of frenzied doctors and nurses rushing around me, the beep of machines monitoring my wellbeing and questions being thrown at me that I couldn't answer. My brain didn't seem capable of processing what was happening. The only thing I knew was that I couldn't feel my legs and I was scared. More than scared. Terrified.

I spent the next few months in the hospital recovering. Every day was a struggle to get that little bit closer to the person I was before the accident. I was reliant on the staff for everything. I'd broken my legs in multiple places. I had to learn how to walk again. It was like being a baby only I had the frustration of knowing just how easy it used to be to put one foot in front of the other.

I'm a naturally optimistic person, but that sunny outlook was sorely tested. I had to constantly remind myself that it could have been so much worse. Although I was in excruciating pain and every day was focused on relearning the most basic of skills, I could have lost my legs. I could have died. I did my best to be grateful for that pain because as long as I could feel something, it meant I was alive and healing.

What no one knew - because I didn't let it show - was how my mind was constantly going over what had happened. I kept asking myself if I could have done anything different to avoid the accident. Why didn't I go a different route? Why didn't I see the pothole?

I was constantly on edge. Due to the nature of my injuries, I had a private room. Every time a nurse, doctor, or therapist opened the door, I jumped, the sudden sound of the door banging open reminding me of the bang of my car's tire blowing out.

At last, the day arrived when I was allowed to go home. On the surface, I seemed happy. Everyone around me was pleased I was leaving the hospital and I didn't want to disappoint them. But inside, I was petrified. Hospital had been the space where I felt safe. Or, at least, knew what to expect. I could trust everyone there. 'Home' was a room in a shared apartment with roommates who were less than friendly. They communicated through passive aggressive notes and had a long list of rules that I struggled to keep up with at the best of times, let alone while recovering from serious injury. I'd moved there only a few weeks before my accident. New to the area, I hadn't had time to make many local friends.

One of my flatmates had a games console and he loved playing a particular racing game. The sound of the screeching tires was torture, but the one time I'd asked him if he could at least turn it down if he couldn't play something else, he snapped at me to go put some earplugs in. Then I had to endure comments about being "the little princess" every time I left my room to get something to eat or drink. If I thought it would make any difference, I'd have told him how I couldn't sleep because the sound of his game made me feel like I was back on the road, powerless to do anything as another car plowed into mine. Instead, I kept quiet, afraid he'd mock me even more. I didn't want to seem weak and I didn't have anywhere else to live. Who would want to live with a mess like me?

This was a month before I broke down. It was completely unpredictable. I'd kept up my positive outlook, always tried to be grateful for everything I had. But the smallest things like doing the washing were a huge chore. I was constantly in pain. The toll it was taking on my physical and mental health left me chronically exhausted. I had no one to call upon to help, so I began spending more and more time locked in my bedroom where I wouldn't be any bother.

It got so bad that I began to wonder whether it would be better for everyone if I wasn't around anymore.

It was my friend, Kelly, who saved my life. She had to come to my city for work so she came to see me while she was here, despite my best efforts to put her off. When she realized how secluded

I'd become, she immediately insisted I flew back home with her to stay.

Once I was surrounded by people who cared for me, it immediately felt like a weight had lifted. I was able to rest without worrying about being triggered by noises from my flatmates' video games or having them getting annoyed with me for not helping with the cleaning.

While I was staying with Kelly I was diagnosed with PTSD. I also had to have more surgeries on my legs which put me back in a wheelchair for a while. However, those surgeries helped correct the damage done to my legs and I'm feeling a lot better now.

Kelly encouraged me to join a support group for PTSD sufferers. Sharing my story and hearing from others really helped me understand that recovery isn't a straightforward path. You'll have setbacks and progress, good days and bad days, but you *do* get better.

Since then I've signed up to various patient engagement projects to help other people who've experienced serious injuries. I've started swimming as part of my therapy and I recently did a long distance swim to raise money for trauma research.

I still get tired easily and I don't know if I'll ever be pain free, but my mental wounds are mostly healed. I have coping mechanisms through therapies, meditation, and mindfulness. After moving back to be closer to my friends, I'm so much happier. I still suffer the occasional flashback and I still don't enjoy driving but I'm getting better. My friends are so supportive and patient with me.

I know I have people I can call when I'm triggered and it makes all the difference.

I'm alive thanks to all those wonderful medics, therapists and friends who cared enough to help. The scars on my legs will never go away, but I'm proud of them now. They tell the story of my recovery.

I've discovered I'm so much stronger than I could ever have believed. I'm living proof that with time and determination, things really do get better.

## YOUR MIND

66  *"Until you make the unconscious conscious, it will direct your life and you will call it fate"* – Jung

It used to be believed that trauma permanently rewired the brain and this damage could not be undone. We now know that this doesn't have to be true. Our brains are highly adaptable and have an ability called neuroplasticity which allows them to form new connections. This means just as trauma rewired your brain to cope with what you went through, you can also rewire your brain to undo the effects of trauma.

Although undoing the impact of trauma will take time and you'll encounter many challenges along the way, you can consciously change how your brain works. You can support it to build new pathways, strengthen the function of certain areas, and develop better connections. It's the same process as any other form of learning.

It is possible to reinforce your prefrontal cortex so you no longer have to be at the whim of flashbacks and irrational thinking. You can build up your hippocampus to improve your memory function. You can calm your hyperactive amygdala to enjoy greater peace of mind. With time and appropriate therapeutic methods, you can restore and improve the functionality of your brain. As such, your recovery, both physically and mentally, does happen largely in your mind.

Your mind is an incredibly powerful organ. Not only does it control your body's movements without you having to consciously think about them, it's also responsible for the mental processes that make you a unique individual. It enables you to plan for the future and remember the past. It shapes your thoughts and, as a consequence, your mindset and outlook.

When your mental health is in good shape, your mind is a wonderful place to be. But when you're suffering from trauma, your mind can be terrifying. As you progress on your healing journey, you'll stumble upon dark days. Days that make you feel worse instead of better. Days when you'll question your decision to begin. Days when your mind might tell you that therapy is a waste of time and you should quit. After all, if you're feeling worse, how can it be that you're healing? Understand that these moments are natural and they will become fewer as you continue to do the work. This understanding will make it easier to be kinder to yourself.

What can you do to ease the pain of these days where you feel discouraged? What are the things that lift your spirits, even a little bit? Would taking a walk in nature to feel the sun on your skin as you leave your cares behind elevate your mood? What about sliding into a hot bath full of Epsom salts where you feel your shoulders relax, your eyelids sink and your mind escape in blissful relief? Do you have friends who will validate you, encourage you, say nice things or just assure you that you matter?

Mindfulness routines are also important inclusions in this list of self-care practices. Whilst the significance of these activities may pale in comparison to the weight of the things causing your disturbance, your healing journey relies on you regularly doing one of your most important jobs – being kind to yourself while your mind and body do the hard work they need to do to heal.

So, take time to consider the activities you'll engage in and the support you're going to need as you embark on this healing journey. You don't have to do this alone. You *could* and you may feel this is your only option. Yes, you could try and tackle everything by yourself but be warned – your mind can be an incredible self-saboteur. You will significantly increase the chance of a successful outcome if you install appropriate support mechanisms. These can be anything from an online support group, an in-person group, a therapist who offers the right therapeutic modality for you, or making sure that the treatments you choose are going to suit your way of thinking and being.

## Identifying your triggers

It's useful to remember that a thought is just a thought. It's not inherently true or false. When you're feeling happy, you can look at yourself in the mirror and think you look amazing. When you're feeling down, you can be wearing exactly the same clothes and look exactly the same way and be bothered by what you see. Neither thought is necessarily true. Rather, highly subjective viewpoints determined, in large part, by how your brain is functioning in that moment.

When you're suffering from PTSD you may experience a flashback, reliving the scene of your trauma, but that's not real. It's not happening at that moment. You're safe. Nothing is harming you. Although, convincing your brain of that can be difficult.

Flashbacks are often caused by what's known as a 'trigger.' These are reminders of your trauma that trick your mind into thinking you're going through the trauma all over again. Triggers may be connected to your experiences, but they can also be tangential. It could be something as seemingly benign as a scent or a sound that allows you to feel the same level of threat you experienced when the original trauma occurred.

You'll remember this from Chapter 4 – triggers, and their consequences, can be highly disruptive. As a counter, it's helpful to identify what they are. Then to put strategies in place for what you will do when they occur. Also what to expect while you're recovering from the consequence of the trigger. In your Workbook you will have mapped out the triggers that are likely to occur in your life. Now, here's a three step process you can use to both identify and disarm your unique triggers:

1. Consequence

    Note what happens when you're triggered.. How do you feel? What emotions are overpowering you? It's okay if you can't name them all - sometimes they're a complex mix that can be tricky to untangle. For example, you might feel angry and sad at the same time or resentful about feeling this way.

In addition to your emotions, note your physical reactions. Is your heart pounding? Are you breathing faster? Does it feel like your blood pressure has shot up? Once you've fully explored the mental and physical sensations associated with your trigger, you'll then be able to pinpoint the triggering event more easily. You'll find space in your Workbook to explore this process.

2. Prelude

Next, think about what happened right before you were triggered. What were you doing? What was happening around you? Was there a specific event or experience that caused you to feel the negative emotions coming over you?

You don't need to feel like there's something wrong with you if the trigger seems to make no sense on the surface. Trauma can cause us to behave irrationally. It may even be that you can't immediately connect the trigger to a traumatizing event because you've blanked out some of the details of what happened from your memory. It might not be until later that you realize that the supposedly happy song that always makes you cry was playing at the time of the initial traumatizing event.

3. Review

Don't worry if you can't fully identify a trigger on your first attempt (or even your fifth or sixth). Keep at it and know that with every try you're getting closer to unlocking the mystery.

Triggers can be complicated so it might take you a while for you to be able to fully explore your trigger, understand its cause and anticipate what's likely to happen as a consequence. Don't be discouraged. The more you do this work, the more self-aware you'll become and as you'll discover later in this book, self-awareness is key to recovering from trauma.

You can't cure a trigger so much as learn how to work with them. After all, they are signals from your mind and body that there is a perceived danger, so they are there to try and protect you. But despite the well-meaning reason behind them, triggers can be frightening, disruptive, and debilitating, which is why it's important to identify what they are and minimize their effect.

Some people prefer to avoid the things that trigger them. This is a perfectly valid choice, but it can hinder your recovery because you're not healing the underlying problems.

As you do the work detailed later in the book, you'll find that your triggers become fewer or may even disappear altogether. You may be able to face the things that were so difficult for you. But at this stage, we're aiming to be able to cope with them while you work on healing your trauma. Later in this book we'll look at further strategies for handling triggers.

## Responding to triggers

If you can, avoid reacting immediately when you feel triggered. Instead, take a break to process how you're feeling. If you can remove yourself from the situation, do so. If this isn't possible, try closing your eyes and focusing on your breath as you inhale and exhale deeply. Remind yourself that the threat is only in your perception by saying to yourself *in this moment I am safe. In this moment everything is fine.* If you were triggered by something someone said, try to paraphrase what they said and repeat it back to them to buy yourself some time to calm down and think of a rational response.

Acknowledge your feelings. Repressing them will only result in them coming up at another time when it may not be appropriate. Do not judge yourself for feeling this way. Whatever emotion is coming up for you is perfectly valid even if you might think of it as irrational. Logic does not enter the equation when it comes to triggers. You might like to journal about how you feel to fully process them. We've created space for you to do this in your Workbook. You might like to carry the Workbook with you so you can do this as close to the time of triggering as possible.

If you find yourself being triggered a lot or that the triggers are simply too much to deal with, seek professional help. Even if you've managed to get them under control, it could well be that a qualified professional will be able to help you refine your coping strategies so they are even more effective. You'll find a review of some of the most common forms of therapy for PTSD later in this book.

You may find it helpful to compile a list of self-care strategies to draw upon after being triggered. These will be unique to you and should include anything you find replenishing. There is space to do this in your Workbook. You may like to share this list with someone you trust, such as a friend, family member, or therapist, so they can support you in your self-care.

Triggers can be emotionally exhausting and debilitating. They often bring with them physical responses and if you've been neglecting your body's needs this can make your triggers worse. Hunger, dehydration, and fatigue may make your trauma responses worse, so make sure you're eating and drinking regularly. Some people find that their mental state is such that they forget to eat, so you could set reminders on your phone to make sure you're having proper meals or nutritious snacks.

## YOUR ANXIOUS THOUGHTS

When I was at my lowest, I was tormented by my anxious thoughts. I focused on the worst case scenario. I obsessed over the past. I was overthinking future possibilities. My mind was performing all sorts of mental gymnastics to avoid dealing with the reality of what was happening right in front of me. It was stopping me from being present. They were nothing but memories of moments long since gone, mind saboteurs attempting to drag me back to the sense of hopelessness I felt when I was going through a traumatic experience - but man, did they feel real.

If you're suffering from anxious thoughts, you'll know that they are difficult to navigate and they can make recovering from trauma similarly difficult. My anxiety made me think that the trauma cycles that were my constant companion for so long were inevitable and the only way of being. They made it hard to trust new people and experiences because they fooled me into thinking that nothing was going to change. I was going to continue to suffer in the same way I had in the past. It was just life and I had to accept it. But it wasn't life. It was a lie.

Those anxious thoughts were bullies I couldn't escape.

It wasn't until I started working with Anna that I was able to get a new perspective. If someone was treating my best friend like this, I'd stand up to them. So why was I letting my thoughts treat *me* like this?

We'll explore further into what you can do to change your thinking later in the book. For now, it's important you know that just because your mind thinks something, that doesn't make it important or true. Remember, your thoughts can often lie to you. If you give credence to everything your mind tells you, you feed those anxious thoughts.

This behavior is not unique to you. It's normal. People who don't suffer from trauma also have negative thoughts. Our minds are programmed to warn us about potential dangers because they're trying to keep us safe.

But just because your mind is capable of performing what is, at times, a helpful function does not mean that the thoughts it produces whilst performing that function are always helpful. Nor do they deserve all of your attention at the exclusion of thoughts generated from a calm, objective, rested mind.

So when you produce a thought that suggests you're going to experience more trauma, pause for a moment to consider the nature and origins of the thought. Perhaps this thought doesn't need your attention. If you produce the thought "I'll never get over my trauma", your objective mind can respond with a similarly powerful thought – "Many others have. I can too".

You might not be able to control all of your thoughts, but you can control the ones you choose to create.

## SCREW WHAT OTHERS THINK

It's important you know that this is your journey. You're the one taking it. Not your thoughts. Not other people. You. If you ever needed permission to be selfish, here it is. It's time to put yourself and your needs first. Quite frankly, screw what anyone else thinks. The only person who matters now is you.

Trauma changed you to the person you are today. Healing is going to change you again. Change is a natural part of life. It's the only constant. We all change and grow. It's human nature. But for those of us who've experienced trauma, that change can be far more dramatic than for others.

You *will* be a different person by the time you come out of the other end of this tunnel. The light is there, waiting for you to travel towards it. You may discover aspects of yourself you buried a long time ago or discard parts of you that you don't need any more. This will be a process of self-discovery unlike anything else you've been through.

It may be that your trauma turned you into a people pleaser to avoid getting hurt again and now you're ready to discover the empowering feeling that comes with the word 'no.' Or maybe you've isolated yourself, held yourself back from forming relationships because you felt unworthy of love. It's time to learn that you *are* worthy and you *are* deserving.

*I wish I could say that to you in person.*

I feel that I have to warn you that you might lose friends along the road to recovery. This can feel like another form of trauma as people you thought would always be there for you decide they don't want you in their life any more.

There are many reasons why this might happen, none of which are your fault. It may be that some people can't cope with what comes up as you process your trauma and move on. They may have been through their own trauma but aren't ready to deal with it yet. Perhaps they were using you because they enjoyed taking advantage of your people pleasing nature and now you're setting boundaries you're no longer useful to them. You may discover - like I did - that your party lifestyle was an attempt to run away from trauma and as you deal with your trauma, your need to party falls away. It could be that all you had in common with your party friends was that you all enjoyed a 'good' time and now you're on different paths, there's nothing to connect you any more.

I wish I could say something trite like 'those people weren't your friends in the first place' but that isn't necessarily true. It may well be that you were incredibly close at one time, which is what makes losing them all the more painful. Sadly, not everyone can cope with the healing process and will want you to stay in the same place because it's comfortable for _them_. For the sake of your health, you can't do that any more. You owe it to yourself to heal so you can be your authentic self, free from trauma. I promise you that for all the friends you lose during this time, you will make new ones, ones who will love you for who you are. Friends that are supportive of how you choose to live a trauma-free life.

To make the change a little easier (or a lot), I personally recommend the LearnWell Community.

This journey isn't meant to be comfortable. And you aren't meant to limit yourself to please those around you. Now is the time to let go of caring about what others think about you. (After all, they're just thoughts. What someone else thinks about you has no real bearing on reality.) Keep your focus on the endgame - your ultimate healing and recovery. Right now, that *has* to be your priority.

No two people are the same. Each person's trauma is unique. Even if you went through exactly the same experience as someone else, the way you responded to it will be very different. Therefore, your healing will be unique to you. Become comfortable with that notion before you start getting uncomfortable while you heal. The healing journey is unpredictable. Things will come up you couldn't have anticipated and you'll probably find that healing brings up a lot more for you to process than one traumatic event. This is why it's important to be prepared for all the possibilities we've covered in this book and have mechanisms put in place to help you handle whatever comes up.

Now, and every time you find yourself feeling uncomfortable about the journey ahead, is a great time to review what you wrote in your Workbook for Chapter 5 – the compelling reason you're on this journey.

In the next chapter we're going to talk about systems and why they're more helpful to you than goals in this process. We'll look at how you can map out your recovery to make it easier for you to implement your chosen therapies and tools.

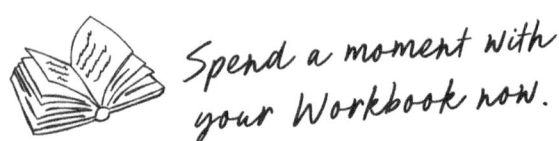 *Spend a moment with your Workbook now.*

**7**

I love this chapter. If your healing could be displayed on a graph, this would be the point where the line turns and heads up and to the right.

# SYSTEMS ARE BETTER THAN GOALS

## How To Build Your Plan For Recovery

*"You do not rise to the level of your goals. You fall to the level of your systems. Your goal is your desired outcome. Your system is the collection of daily habits that will get you there."*

- James Clear

## FINN'S STORY:

My life changed forever one dark October night. I was wearing a dark overcoat, a decision I'll always regret. I was crossing the road to get to my car when a driver plowed into me. I was knocked out so I don't remember what happened next, but I later learned that I'd been sent flying, landing on the opposite side of the road due to the force of the impact.

I was rushed to hospital where they thought I was going to die. I'd broken my neck, my spine, my shoulder, my ribs, my pelvis ... It's probably easier to list the bones that *weren't* broken! The consultant who operated on me said that my injuries were akin to ones he'd seen while working in Iraq, treating soldiers caught up in bomb blasts. My family were warned to expect the worst. They were even asked to consider donating my organs.

Somehow, they patched me up enough to survive, but that was just the start of a long, slow process back to wellness.

I was kept in a medically induced coma for two weeks. When I woke up, I was dazed and disoriented. I tried to talk around the pipe down my throat to ask what had happened, but a garbled mess came out. They gave me a pen and paper to write out what I wanted to say, but all I could produce was a scribble. It took a few days for my brain to unscramble enough for me to understand what had happened.

My memories of that period are foggy. I remember hearing people crying and thinking they were crying because I'd died. I tried to call out to say that I was fine but all that came out was a croak. When my girlfriend, Alexis, finally realized what I was trying to say, she did her best to reassure me, but I was convinced that if I wasn't dead then I must be dying but nobody was brave enough to tell me the truth.

It was the support of my family and friends that got me through that time. The hospital staff were understanding and turned a blind eye to visiting hours at times when I was particularly stressed. The nurses were lovely. I wish I could say the same about physical therapy. My therapist was perfectly pleasant, but if I thought the pain of the accident was bad, it was nothing compared to how it felt while they were working on my body to undo the damage caused by the accident.

I was assigned a nurse who specialized in trauma - Clare*. She was the one who helped me put together a plan for my recovery.

Clare explained that if I wanted to give myself the best chance of a full recovery, I needed to decide what my ideal outcome would look like and how to make it happen. At the same time, she warned me to let go of any sense of time. Recovery would occur when I was ready and not a moment before. She told me that's why the people in her care were called patients. Our job was literally to be patient!

This was probably the hardest part of recovery for me. I was so frustrated at how long everything took. I wanted to know exactly when I'd be able to walk without crutches, when I could go climbing, when I could go on holiday, when I could get back to work and so on. But all anyone could tell me was that it would happen eventually.

Eventually, I did get one date that was set in stone: 14th February, the day I was allowed to go home. It was also the day I proposed to my girlfriend. I will always be grateful for the way she looked after me and having her by my side during the darkest days convinced me that she was the woman I wanted with me for the rest of my life. With everything we've been through together, I know nothing can ever come between us.

Alexis became my full time carer. Fortunately, she worked online so was able to fit work around the support I needed. She became my private physical therapist, working through the exercises we'd been shown to help me recover my mobility.

She was also with me during those sleepless nights when I woke up screaming.

I find it hard to drive anywhere . I'm on constant high alert for accidents. Since I can't drive myself, I'm always the passenger and the lack of control adds an extra layer of fear to the experience. One of the goals on my long-term plan is to do one of those racing car experiences, just so I can prove to myself that my fear doesn't own me.

When you're in a serious accident, you're often so focused on the physical trauma, you overlook the mental impact. I later found out that I should have had support for my mental health a lot earlier in my recovery. I still struggle with insomnia and go through very dark periods. I wasn't able to go back to work which was a real blow. I loved my job as a personal trainer, but it was impossible for me to coach anyone while I could barely walk from one side of the room to another.

Intead, Alexis helped me put together some online fitness programs. I plan out the courses and she's the model demonstrating the techniques. She's taught me a lot about online marketing and I'm making more money now than I did before my accident.

As part of my recovery plan, Alexis and I put together a bucket list. Top of the list was to visit the seven natural wonders. We've booked a trip to go see the Northern Lights for our honeymoon. Yes, we've set a date to get married! We also plan to go swimming with sharks and walk over hot coals. I want to challenge myself, prove that the accident hasn't stopped me doing anything.

I'm currently in talks to film a documentary about my recovery. I want to share my story so other trauma sufferers know they're not alone. I also want people to learn from my experience so they can heal more effectively. Much as I'm eternally grateful to all the people who treated me and helped get me where I am today, there are things that could have been done differently that would have better supported my recovery. I was given blood at the scene of the accident which saved my life, but if I'd had better psychological support earlier, maybe I wouldn't have to work so hard now to deal with my PTSD. A more coordinated approach between the various departments I worked with would have helped things run more smoothly.

The plan I drew up with Clare made a huge difference though. On days when I'm feeling low, I look back over it to remind myself how far I've come. I've been told that it's going to take another 12 months of physical therapy before I can be signed off. I'm always going to have the scars to remind me not to wear dark clothing at night.

But I'm also going to have Alexis by my side.

I take each day as it comes. And I'm grateful to be alive. Everything else is a bonus.

## YOUR NEW LIFESTYLE

Today is indeed the first day of the rest of your life. Consider your trauma recovery as the next chapter in your life, an opportunity to envision and create a happier, healthier lifestyle.

What would an ideal day look like in a life free from trauma? What would be different? How would you look? How would you walk? How would you talk? Who would you talk with? What would you eat? Where would you work? How would you feel?

Today, you have the opportunity to create whatever you want for the rest of your life. Of course, this is not unique to those who have experienced trauma. Anyone can do this. However, your trauma has given you a reason to consider how you want to live and how you want to change. Many people don't have a reason to pause and reflect on their life so they continue on as life would lead them. You, on the other hand, are in the seat of creation and anything you can dream is possible for you.

Go to your Workbook now to visualize and document your dream. You'll find prompts in there to provoke your thinking and the final result will be your compelling future. Do that now and return here once you're finished.

You've now got a dream that lights you up and draws you to action. Brilliant! Now what ... ?

Well, ordinary wisdom would suggest mantras, vision boards, and goal-setting techniques. All of which have a place but it's only a small part of your outcome.

Where your momentum and ultimate success are going to emerge is from what you do every day. Your daily, consistent activities are what will get you closer to, or further from, your ideal life.

## PUT IN PLACE SYSTEMS TO SUPPORT YOUR VISION

Once you're clear on where you want to be, your systems will move you towards them. In the subsequent sections of this book, you'll find several tools and strategies you can use to heal from trauma. You'll choose the ones which resonate with you or which are accessible to you. Not all therapies are available in all areas, which may be a factor in your decisions.

We often overestimate what we can do in the short term but underestimate what we can achieve in the long term. Trauma can be caused by a single, major event, but we don't need a big, defining moment to undo it. Your small, incremental changes on a daily basis might be subtle or even unnoticeable, but in time they are what make the biggest difference. A 1% reduction in the severity of your symptoms every day will ensure that you're in a significantly better place in a year's time. Little setbacks along the way won't undermine that progress if you follow your systems and have faith in them.

Your experience to this point might have convinced you that you're broken. That's so untrue. Your trauma symptoms are the evidence of your mind and body trying to keep you safe. The reason why you haven't been able to detach from them is not that you're defined by your trauma but simply because you haven't had the right system for change... until now.

It's time to start believing new things about yourself. You are a survivor. You are someone who has lived through some extreme experiences but you're still here to tell the tale. The systems you put in place need to support this new survivor mentality backed up with a belief that you are worthy of everything you want.

So this is your moment to decide who you want to be. Are you going to continue to allow your trauma to determine your course? Or are you going to fix your focus on your new vision and establish the habits required to make it your new reality?

If you chose your new reality then it's time to prove it to yourself. It's time to take your first steps towards it by adopting new tools, every day as part of your new system. This is your opportunity to build your new identity. Every step forward is evidence that you *can* do it.

## HOW TO BUILD YOUR NEW SYSTEMS

In your Workbook there is a tool designed that incorporates your new 'system' for achieving your ideal life. It will become an extremely powerful resource. Turn to it as you need but, for now, I'll explain some of the things you'll be using.

Once you've completed this book, you'll have an awareness of the vast array of resources available to support you on your healing journey. Of course, you won't do everything. You'll do those things that appeal to you and are available.

It may not be hard to choose between the options presented but just choosing is not where the transformation happens. It's only in turning up that any difference is made and turning up is the hardest part. So, your system will comprise not just choices but times, locations, and even a backup for when you don't turn up.

In your Workbook you'll see the following decision patterns:

**Commitment:** I will [do X] at [Y time] at [Z place].

This expresses a commitment to do something. The usual pattern is "I'm going to attend a healing session". That's wonderful but without a time or a place, it remains an idea. Not a commitment. With an activity, a time, and a place, it's a commitment.

**Backup:** If I [don't do X], then I will [Y]

Sometimes things just don't go to plan. Even commitments! So, a backup is required. For each commitment you make, you'll be invited to create a backup to ensure that missing a commitment doesn't mean that you miss out altogether. You default to your backup plan. For example, "If I don't attend the session then I will reschedule for the next available session".

When you build your system, you will create your commitments and backup plans to ensure that the choices you make become the actions you take. This will also relate to the vision of your life you created earlier. For each of those sections, you'll make a commitment to an action at a time and, where possible, a place so that you have meaningful steps planned to bring that vision to life.

Your plan will then comprise a weekly collection of activities that will become your healing journey. You can reprint this each month and recommit to those things that are proving useful and experiment with other options you may not have tried.

So turn now to your Workbook to see how your system works. You'll then return here to continue on to the next part, where the rubber really meets the road.

# PART 3

## Tools

We've explored deeply into how trauma pervades every aspect of your life. You may not have realized just how much trauma has shaped your life and how it influences every thing you do.

But now you know how invasive trauma can be, it's time to untangle its threads from your life. We'll do that through the work of healing.

While it may be hard work, that doesn't mean it can't at times be fun or enjoyable. Many of the resources I'll give you are activities that are pleasurable in their own right. In rebuilding your life to be free of trauma, there's a high probability that you'll end up with a lifestyle that's better than you ever thought possible.

I'll give you several ways to move forward and you'll choose which path you take.

# LAYING THE FOUNDATIONS FOR HEALING

Two Simple Ways You Can Do
The Groundwork For Recovery

*Change happens by doing small things consistently.*

## JENNIFER'S STORY:

I used to be one of *those* people. You know, the ones who'd read about abused women being murdered by their partners and think *if it was that bad, why didn't she just leave?*

You can't understand until it happens to you.

When I first met my husband, he was the most wonderful man I'd ever known. I know now that this is what they call love bombing. He made me feel like a queen. I was the most important woman in the world to him and I knew that once we were married, we were going to spend the rest of our lives making each other happy. I was half right.

Once that ring was on my finger, everything changed. It was subtle at first, little comments here and there. A dig at my weight. A remark about the length of my skirt. I found myself working hard to maintain my appearance to keep Nathan* happy. The harder I tried to please him, the less successful I became.

Over time, he stopped me going out with my friends. Not directly. Oh no. He would just refuse to come out with us and be in such a foul mood when I came home that it was easier to pass on any invites that came my way until the invites dried up. Then Nathan insisted we move to another city, far away from my family. He said that there were better job opportunities and it would be a fresh start for both of us. We could build the life we wanted, just the two of us.

The first time he hit me, I blamed myself. I should have known he'd be worried about me when I was working late. He was so sweet afterwards, I believed him when he said it would never happen again. I look back and laugh at how naive I was.

When I fell pregnant, I thought the beatings would stop. He was so clever, making sure never to leave bruises where anyone could see, but I felt sure he wouldn't risk hurting our baby.

Instead, it got worse. Nathan accused me of having an affair. He said he couldn't possibly be the father. He called me all sorts of names and swore he'd make sure I'd never be able to have kids.

He started hitting me, each blow getting harder. Usually, I'd just curl up and take it, knowing it would soon be over. This time, I had a baby to protect, so I did something I'd never dared to do before: I hit back.

Big mistake.

I thought Nathan was going to kill me. The blows rained down like hailstorms. I tried to get away, but I tripped and fell down the stairs.

When I woke up, I was in the ICU. It turned out that one of my neighbors had heard my screams and called the police. They were able to get to me before Nathan finished the job the stairs had started. To this day, I firmly believe he would have killed me if the police hadn't stopped him.

By some miracle, the baby survived, but I was in bad shape. Nathan had left me with life-changing injuries. I'll never be able to walk without limping and I have a metal plate in my head that always sets off the scanners whenever I fly anywhere.

If it had only been broken bones, I might have been okay. But every time I closed my eyes, I could see his face up against mine, his enraged snarl as he accused me of all sorts of terrible things. Even though he was safely behind bars, I wasn't free. He still kept me prisoner in my own mind.

That wasn't the only problem. Nathan had been financially abusive too. I didn't have my own bank account or money. Our apartment was rented in his name. I hadn't been allowed to have a car. I was effectively destitute.

I was lucky. One of the nurses at the hospital put me in touch with a charity for abused women and they arranged for some emergency funding to get me back on my feet. They also paid for one of my friends to fly out to visit so I didn't have to be alone.

That support in the early stages of my recovery was invaluable. I knew I was racking up huge medical bills, but the charity assured me not to worry. They could help me figure something out and there were grants available for women like me.

It was months before I was ready to leave the hospital, but the charity had assigned me a caseworker who helped me get back on my feet. I decided to move back home to be near my family for the birth of my baby.

I'm so glad I got away. I was having flashbacks, waking up at night in the middle of a panic attack because I thought Nathan had found me. Even when he was sent to prison for attempted murder, I couldn't shake the feeling that he was stalking me.

The charity arranged for me to get financial advice so I could start rebuilding my finances after years with no credit rating. They also put me in touch with domestic abuse support and therapists so I could process what I'd been through.

I did a course for abused women. That taught me so much about how the long-term trauma of living with an abuser had affected me. It was upsetting to find out how common my story was, but I made a lot of friends in that group. Being surrounded by women who'd been through the same as me made me feel I wasn't alone. When I gave birth to my little girl they all got together and bought me supplies for her - diapers, clothes, formula, etc. - so she didn't want for anything.

I'm still a long way off a full recovery, but I take every day as it comes. My beautiful daughter motivates me to keep going through the bad patches. I have a strong support network around me and I know I'm going to be okay. Surviving my husband was just the start. Now I want to thrive.

## Early In The Healing Path Is Education

You won't fully appreciate the immense value of this just now but you need to know that you're several steps along the path of healing. First comes acknowledgment of the trauma, then a decision to act, then education. You're at 'education' which is a stage that very few of even the best-intentioned people get to. Well done.

Further, the level to which you educate yourself about trauma will have a significant impact on how trauma affects your life. The more you can build awareness, both of your PTSD and yourself, the better you'll be able to cope with any negative side effects along the road to recovery - and the better you'll be able to manage your trauma.

One of the most important aspects we lose from our childhood is curiosity. That's why kids are so fearless. Their curiosity overrides their fear. So the more curious you become about yourself, the more you educate yourself, the more your fears will subside. You'll discover you don't need to let your trauma rule your life anymore. You'll find yourself ready to move on.

Let's briefly recap some of the points from earlier chapters.

Trauma occurs when you go through a physically or emotionally harmful event or one which is life-threatening. The impact of the event can continue long after the event has finished. This is, in part, because the traumatic event triggers the release of adrenaline and other stress hormones in the brain, prompting the fight or flight response to help you run away or defend yourself. This is an automatic response designed to keep you alive. At that moment, mental health is not a consideration. Survival is the brain and body's only concern.

When adrenaline is released, the prefrontal cortex is temporarily shut down. This is the part of the brain that deals with executive functions such as decision-making, problem-solving, and self-control, as well as primary cognitive skills like memory, language, emotional expression, and motor control.

Trauma traps that stressful event in the brain, storing the memory of it in the amygdala. This is meant to protect you from being in similar danger again. However, the amygdala stores the trauma as an emotional event experienced by the five senses, so the memory is made up of scraps of sights, sounds, tastes, smells, or sensations. These memories are held in the short-term memory store, which is what causes flashbacks.

Since the trauma is held in the physical body as sensory memories, it can be triggered by any physical or sensory input that mimics the circumstances of the trauma, even if only tangentially. This is why you might be driving with the radio on and when you hear a song it triggers a flashback. The brain remembers the song playing during the time of trauma and misinterprets it as a sign of danger. In chapter six, you were given a process for identifying your triggers. The more you explore your triggers, the more you'll understand that they're your mind trying to protect you, even if it doesn't feel like it. When you're triggered, ask yourself:

- Where was I?

- What was happening?

- How was I feeling?

- What sensory inputs were occurring? (Sights, smells, sounds, tastes, or physical sensations.)

- What was I thinking?

- What was I feeling in my body?

It isn't always possible to avoid triggers, which is why it's so important to know what they are so you can learn how to deal with them. Understanding what triggers you will also help you understand why you react the way you do. This will help you feel more in control because your triggers will feel less random and have a certain level of predictability to them.

Later in this book, we'll go over a number of strategies you can use to handle your triggers.

It is important you understand that everyone experiences trauma differently. What's triggering for me may not be for you. This is why this book doesn't take a one-size-fits-all approach. It's more of a toolkit filled with tools that are helpful in the right circumstances. It's no good using a hammer when you really need a screwdriver. It's up to you to determine what tool is best for your circumstances. Take your time to experiment until you find the ones that work. Be reassured that there *will* be a way of healing your trauma. You've come so far already. Now's the time to take those final steps.

## Build Your Support Network

Nobody should have to deal with trauma alone. Yet many people needlessly feel ashamed about their trauma and feel that they can't talk about it with their existing network.

### You Have Nothing To Be Ashamed Of

At the same time, I know how hard it can be to open up to people, especially when hiding your trauma has been a way of life for so long. All I can say is that if I'd only spoken to Anna sooner - or anyone else for that matter - I could have saved myself a lot of pain. It might be difficult to talk to people, but you're already committed to doing the toughest job there is - getting well. Even if you only choose one person to open up to, it will help relieve you of the burden you've been carrying.

Your network and community are an essential part of the healing process. The company you keep will make a huge difference to your ability to heal. For example, if you're like me, and you're partying hard to blank out your trauma, you may find that this isn't a healthy environment conducive to healing. You might have to make some hard choices about who you keep in your life and who you distance yourself from, at least while you're healing.

Not everyone will be supportive of your decision to heal. Not everyone is altruistic and not everyone likes to see people improving. There will be those who dismiss your experiences or who simply won't want to hear about your progress. This can be incredibly hurtful, especially when it comes from someone you least expect to react in that way.

Again, this is where you'll need to be strong. Establish firm boundaries and make it clear that your healing is non-negotiable. If someone is not willing to be there for you while you recover, you are not obliged to keep them around.

So make a decision. Look around at your family, friends, and colleagues. Who can you bring into your healing network? Who do you need to keep at a distance? The kind of network we're talking about can't be bought or outsourced. It's up to you to attract the right people to support you.

You might decide you don't want to include your colleagues in this process. You may feel it would undermine your professionalism to be open with them about your experiences. Conversely, you may feel you'll do a better job if you can make people aware of what you've had to deal with and what might come up while you're healing. It may be you'll need to take some mental health days, so you might feel you should warn your team about the possibility.

Only you can determine how much your colleagues need to know, if anything.

Your family can be a problematic part of this process. It may be that they're the cause of your trauma. Sometimes your family's response to your trauma can make things worse too. They may gaslight you or not believe you when you tell them what happened. It might be they feel guilty that they allowed you to go through this but rather than owning up to their part in your experiences, they victim blame and cause even more trauma.

Of course, it may be that your family is there for you 100%. They've loved and cared for you your whole life. They're going to want to hold your hand as you travel along the road to healing. You simply can't know until you talk to them.

Unless you're estranged from your family, it's always worth at least testing the waters with them to see how understanding they'll be of what you're going through. Try telling them about your experiences if they don't already know and let them know what you need from them. You may be pleasantly surprised by their reaction. If not, you can at least take heart from the fact you've tried and turn to others to build your support network.

Unlike family, you choose your friends. So you'd expect your friends to be there for you when you need, right?

Well, sometimes. As I've already touched upon, not all friends have your best interests at heart. Some are more invested in you staying ill. Like 'Fun Bobby' in *Friends,* they may find you more interesting when you're under the influence of drugs or alcohol and complain that you're 'boring' now you're trying to get well.

These are not the people you need with you as you travel down the road to healing. Maybe you'll be able to reconnect with them once you're better. Maybe they were those friends who came into your life for a season (rather than reason or lifetime), and it's time to let them go. This is the time for you to put your own needs and well-being first and let go of anyone who isn't a true friend.

A true friend will want the best for you. They'll be there when you need them. They'll wipe away your tears or go with you to a yoga class. You may find that when you start thinking about who you can rely on for emotional support during the healing process you end up with a very short list and that's okay. Even if your list has just one name on it, you can take heart that you're not alone.

While there's nothing like an in-person discussion, you can look into online support groups that will let you talk about your feelings and experiences. It may be that you find local people there who you can meet up with. There may also be local groups you can attend. If you're having problems with drugs or alcohol you can look at groups like Alcoholics Anonymous or Narcotics Anonymous.

You don't have to look for support in trauma-related groups. You might make good friends at activities you take up as part of your recovery. Look into local yoga or meditation classes. See if there are any ice bathing or ocean dip groups where you can swim in cold water together. Maybe there are community volunteering groups or church organizations you can join.

You may want to find single-gender groups to connect with, especially if you've had a traumatic experience with the opposite gender. There are some benefits to being among people of the same gender. While it is a generalization and there are always exceptions, men and women tend to process trauma differently. Men may be more likely to feel anger and lash out, while women tend to become anxious and depressed - as well as be more likely to develop PTSD.[1] This may affect how you express yourself and how easily others find it to genuinely listen to what you're saying.

If you think that it will be easier for you to open up to people of the same gender, don't be afraid to seek out gender-specific support groups. Right now, all that matters is you get the help you need, whatever form that takes.

You never know who you're going to meet who's had a similar experience to you and who will help you along the way. All you have to do is create the intention to meet people. It's amazing who comes into your life when you do.

## Safe Relationships Will Help You Heal

The concept of 'safety' in relationships is what enables us to connect, open up, be vulnerable, and allow healing. Some people naturally make us feel safe but it can take time to build that relationship with others. Safe relationships are priceless, not only because they allow us to be open about our experiences and really explore what's going on inside our immensely complex brains, but also because they help us feel grounded and, well, safe.

A safe relationship with someone can help regulate our nervous systems.[2] Where our bodies are used to being filled with adrenaline and cortisol, someone who makes us feel safe gives us a chance to rest. It tells our bodies that it's okay to relax and be free from the state of fight or flight.

There are a number of identifying features of a safe relationship. Look for these if you're unsure whether you can open up to someone:

- **Predictability.** The other person behaves in such a way that we know what to expect from them. They're there when they say they will. They mean what they say and say what they mean. This makes it easier for our bodies to relax out of fight or flight because we know where we stand.

- **Constant warmth.** When someone is always warm and kind towards us, we are more inclined to build strong bonds with them. If someone blows hot and cold, we don't know how they feel towards us and it's harder to let down our guard.

- **A lack of judgment.** Regardless of their personal opinions, we feel safe when we know we can share our thoughts and feelings with them without being judged.

- **Discernment.** As you process your trauma, your behavior might be erratic. Someone makes us feel safe when we know they can separate what we *do* from who we *are*. They understand that when we lash out it's not personal.

(Although they're also able to maintain boundaries. It's a sad irony that we often hurt the ones we love the most because we feel safe enough to let down the walls because we know they're not going anywhere. Try not to take advantage of your trusted relationships like this or you may find you push people away.)

- **Empathy.** Some people prefer to deal with other trauma survivors because they know they've been through the same experience. There's a lot to be said for knowing someone understands you because of their history. But someone who's empathetic can feel your pain without having been through trauma. Knowing they understand how you feel will make it easier to open up.

- **Validation.** Building on the previous point, it's important you feel supported, accepted, and seen. Knowing that you're not alone and you're not mad goes a long way toward helping you process your past.

- **Sensitivity.** Supporting someone through trauma is a difficult job. There will be times when someone in your inner circle makes a mistake or doesn't get things right. It's how they handle these situations that makes all the difference. If they own their mistakes and do their best to put things right, you can feel that you matter and your well-being is important.

- **Wisdom.** Sometimes an objective second opinion really helps us to gain perspective. When you have someone you feel safe with giving you advice, you know that it's okay to listen to their advice. It may be that your trauma is making you act out in ways you can't recognize. A safe person can help you see where you're crossing a line and support you to find healthier ways of interacting.

- **An ability to be comfortable with feelings.** The chances are you've been bottling up your feelings for far too long, either because you were punished for expressing your emotions or because you felt an erroneous sense of shame about them due to your trauma. It's important you can feel safe enough to express more extreme emotions such as sadness, anger, grief, fear, anxiety, or depression so you can process and heal them.

Your Workbook will help you get your network in place, or at least help to create the process of putting it together. Then you can start looking at what tools you're going to use. We'll examine how you can prepare yourself for therapy in the next chapter.

# RESOURCING

## How To Find Your Happy Place

*Comedy acts as my therapy. I put my problems out there. I talk about them. I talk about everything before anybody has a chance.*

— *Kevin Hart*

## LAURIE'S STORY:

I was abused by my grandfather when I was a child. I didn't tell anyone. He was popular in the community. He used to be Santa Claus at the local youth center. He was always volunteering. Everyone thought he was a real stand-up guy. Only I knew the truth, but who would believe me?

I started self-harming when I was 10, smoking when I was 11 and by the time I was 12 I was regularly stealing drinks from my parents' liquor cabinet and smoking dope whenever I could persuade one of the older kids to let me. Sometimes I performed sex acts so I could get a hit.

I was a total mess.

I ended up having a mental breakdown when I was in my late teens. I was committed to a psych ward which turned out to be the best thing that could have happened to me. I was finally able to tell my story and know that I was believed. I was supported through my recovery.

But then the day came when I was told I was going to be discharged. I was terrified. I'd been safe in hospital. What was going to happen to me out in the big bad world?

I didn't want to go home. I had too many traumatic memories of what had happened there. Instead, I was placed in a halfway house while I went to community college to get my high school diploma.

Before my release, I sat down with my therapist to put together some coping strategies. I'd learned a lot of techniques while I was in hospital like mindfulness and focusing on my breath. We came up with some ideas for what I could do when I was feeling overwhelmed. I also had the number of a helpline I could call if I felt like I needed extra support.

Just knowing I had that number made a lot of difference. I didn't call, but it was a great comfort to know there was always someone at the end of the phone if I needed to talk.

I got my high school diploma and now I'm training to be a therapist. I want to help people like me so they don't have to feel alone.

## GATHERING YOUR RESOURCES

Let's say you've found a great therapist, one who makes you feel safe and holds space for you while you explore your feelings. You've chosen a therapeutic approach that works for you and you feel like you're making progress during that one hour a week you have with your therapist.

What do you do for the other 167 hours?

This is where resourcing is so important. You need more than just therapy to be able to navigate your daily life. Having coping strategies that suit your needs will help you take an active role in your healing.

Humans have an almost limitless capacity to redefine themselves as they search for self-fulfillment. But when you're knee-deep in trauma you can lose sight of this. You can feel lost, helpless, alone and hopeless. It's easy to forget that however bad you feel, you always have unlimited potential for growth. When you give yourself a range of support mechanisms, it can help sustain you through dark times because you always have something to lean on when you need.

The more resources you have at your fingertips, the better equipped you are to handle your trauma. Therapy is one resource. It's a safe space in which you can work on developing your other resources. A good therapist will help you recognize that you're more resourceful than you may have realized.

Resources can fall into five categories that you can pick and choose from to help yourself negotiate the healing process:

1. **Functional.** These are the practicalities of self-care and looking after yourself. They may include a safe home and/or somewhere to go to recharge and recuperate; healthy food or comfort food; practical activities that give you a sense of achievement such as arts and crafts; hobbies or daily activities that give your life meaning and help you feel productive; self-care activities that nurture your spirit such as having a massage, taking a relaxing bath, having a manicure or haircut, or spending time in the sunshine.

2. **Physical.** Activities that involve moving the body in some way, such as team sports, going to the gym, working out, dancing, or running.

3. **Psychological.** Activities that use intelligence, logic, problem solving, humor, or provide an outlet for creative abilities. You might like to find your happy place -

somewhere real or imagined that engenders a feeling of calm, peace, relaxation, or even bliss.

4. **Interpersonal.** In the previous chapter, we talked about the importance of a support network. You can add people to this network who you might not necessarily want to discuss your trauma with, but who you enjoy spending time with and who lift your mood just by being there. This can include our furry friends as well as people.

5. **Spiritual.** This includes religious or non-religious practices, including prayer, meditation, mindfulness, spending time in nature, listening to music, reading poetry, or any other activity you feel nourishes your soul/spiritual side.

You do not need to use resources from every single one of these categories. In fact, it might feel overwhelming or daunting to have to find so many ways to help yourself.

Instead, you might like to start with things that have helped you in the past and then throw in a couple of extra resources that sound interesting. It might be you've never gone for a walk just for the joy of feeling the sun on your skin. Go ahead, see how it makes you feel to walk around the local park or explore the beach. You can never have too many resources. It may be you don't have many or even any because at the time of your trauma you may have been too small to run away or not strong enough to fight off your attacker. You may not have had someone to protect you or simply be too young to understand what was going on. But that was the past. You now have infinite opportunities to find as many resources as you need to support your healing.

Other ideas you mind find helpful include:

- Reading biographies and autobiographies about people who've overcome trauma. It helps a lot to know that others have been where you are and have risen above it. Oprah Winfrey was born into poverty with an abusive family and grew up to be one of the world's richest women. She's a true inspiration.

- Read self-help books about mental health. This book's a great start and there are plenty of others out there to suit all circumstances.

- Read books about psychotherapy. Learning more about how a therapist might approach your situation will help prepare you for what's to come.

- Join self-help groups.

- Watch films or series about therapists or people overcoming adversity and trauma.

In your Workbook, there is space for you to create an index of your resources. This is where you can keep an accumulating written record as you go along. This index will help you keep track of the resources you have at your disposal.

In the next chapter we're going to look at the multitude of avenues available for tackling trauma. You'll discover that you have more choice than you may have thought.

# 10

## STRONG PEOPLE GET HELP

Eleven Types Of Therapy And
How To Choose Between Them

*Real change happens when you get sick of
putting up with your own sh\*t.*

## MARK'S STORY:

When I was a child, I was admitted to hospital with a burst appendix. I needed emergency surgery or I would have died.

I seemed to recover okay. I mean, I was a kid and kids are resilient, right?

But that experience left me with a severe phobia of needles. I couldn't even see one without feeling sick and inducing a panic attack. I couldn't have any vaccinations because I would hyperventilate at the thought of rolling up my sleeve.

I didn't realize I was experiencing a trauma response until I was diagnosed with diabetes when I was 22. I was unusual because I had type 1 diabetes - most people with it get diagnosed much younger, around 13 or 14.

I was going to have to inject myself with insulin every day if I wanted to stay alive. But how could I when I couldn't go near a needle?

When I mentioned this to my doctor, she suggested I might be suffering from trauma. At first, I didn't want to believe her. I wasn't crazy. I just didn't like needles! But my girlfriend at the time persuaded me to go and see a psychologist and that's when I was diagnosed with PTSD. My therapist explained that my childhood illness had embedded negative thought processes in my mind so now whenever I was confronted with needles it triggered a fight or flight response.

After an initial assessment, my psychologist recommended I try a form of therapy called EMDR. It sounded weird - you move your eyes from left to right while thinking about a traumatic experience - but I knew that if I didn't deal with my needle phobia I could suffer severe health issues or possibly die. I figured I had nothing to lose and everything to gain, so I agreed to try.

Over the course of eight weeks, I sat with my therapist and relived my time in hospital as a child while my eyes tracked her finger moving from left to right. At first, it was deeply uncomfortable. It felt like I was back in the hospital as a small boy, helpless and scared.

But over time, the memory had less and less of a hold over me. I could talk about what happened without tears pricking at my eyes.

By the time my therapy was over, I no longer had a problem with needles. I was able to dose myself with life-saving insulin without any hesitation. I even got a tattoo - an image of a syringe to remind me how far I've come!

## WHAT THERAPY DO YOU NEED?

Remember how I mentioned the importance of education? If you don't know all your options, you might feel under pressure to simply go along with whatever your therapist recommends rather than coming to the discussion with a working knowledge of the most popular therapies and playing an active role in deciding which one is best.

I'm going to talk you through some of the most popular treatments for trauma, the ones with the highest success rate. Note that everyone is different so you can't guarantee that a particular treatment will work for you. You'll hear some people say that EMDR has a 100% success rate, for example, yet through trauma support groups, I know that it doesn't suit everyone. Some people find it makes their flashbacks worse because they're reliving the trauma but it isn't moving into their long-term memory the way it's supposed to.

Remember - you don't have to stick with a particular therapy if you don't feel it's working for you. That doesn't mean you should jump from one to another without giving them a chance. It does take time to heal the damage caused by years of trauma, so you're not going to get instant results. But there will be a treatment that suits you. Doing your research beforehand will give you the best possible chance of getting it right the first time.

As you read through these forms of therapy, you're encouraged to take notes on each. There is space in your Workbook dedicated to this. Your notes will form a helpful source of summarized information to refer to as you decide which form of therapy may be most appropriate for you.

## EMDR

Paul's story:

*When my therapist first recommended EMDR to me I was skeptical. I mean, it sounds ridiculous! How can looking from left to right and back again while thinking about your trauma change anything? Whoever came up with it has a very interesting way of thinking! Yet it really does work.*

*My therapist had a device with disks you held in each hand while they pulsed alternately. I found it uncomfortable, so instead, they moved their fingers from side to side while I tracked them with my eyes. They guided me to think about a traumatic event while I was doing this. We'd take a short break to discuss what came up and then repeated the process.*

*I had eight sessions in total. That was two years ago and the effects are still there. I'm no longer bothered by flashbacks and I'm much calmer in myself. I wish I'd learned about EMDR sooner - it's been nothing short of a miracle!*

EMDR was pioneered by Francine Shapiro, an American psychotherapist. When she was a graduate student, she was walking in a park, thinking about a traumatic event she'd experienced. This was a regular occurrence for her. What wasn't so regular was that she realized the memory wasn't having the same negative impact on her.

She thought about what she'd been doing while reliving the memory and determined that the only unusual thing was that her eyes had been moving side to side then diagonally up and down.

Curious as to whether this really was what had made the difference, Shapiro thought about a different difficult memory while moving her eyes. Again, she found that the thoughts lost their intensity.

She shared her discovery with other people at the research center and asked them to try out her new method. They all found that their anxiety about a memory decreased and they became better at dealing with difficult situations. Shapiro ended up doing her doctoral dissertation on her research, publishing her study and method in a professional journal. Other clinicians started doing their studies and using the technique with their patients with promising results.

Since then, numerous randomized controlled studies have all found EMDR to be an effective treatment for PTSD. In fact, the World Health Organization lists EMDR as one of only two recommended psychotherapies for children, adolescents, and adults with PTSD.

## What To Expect From EMDR

There are eight phases to the EMDR process:

1. **History and plan.** Initially, you'll talk about your trauma and how it makes you feel with your therapist before coming up with a treatment plan.

2. **Preparation.** Your therapist will talk you through how EMDR works. You'll decide on the best way to approach bilateral stimulation. For most people, this will involve moving the eyes from side to side, either following the therapist's fingers or a light on a bar. However, there are alternatives if you find it hard to move your eyes, such as holding a device in each hand that delivers pulses to alternate sides or tapping each knee in turn.

3. **Assessment.** You will choose the memory at the heart of your emotional distress to focus on. Your therapist will also take you through imagery and stress reduction techniques you can use both during and after your sessions.

4. **Desensitization.** You will focus on the chosen memory while moving your eyes or engaging in another form of bilateral stimulation. As you work through the memory, you may find that new thoughts, feelings, images, or body sensations come up, the memory losing its negative associations.

5. **Installation.** You will then connect your memory with a new, positive belief. For example, "I am strong. I am capable," instead of the previous belief of "It was all my fault."

6. **Body scan.** You will think about your trauma while scanning your body to see how it feels and observe if you still feel the same about the thought as you did before EMDR.

7. **Closure.** At the end of the session, you'll discuss what's going to happen at the next session as well as exploring what you can do to cope with any feelings or new memories that may crop up before your next session.

8. **Re-evaluation.** At the beginning of the next session, you'll discuss your current mental state to see whether the treatment is still working and look at any new memories that may have arisen since your last session.

EMDR sessions usually last between 60–90 minutes. You are always in control of the process and can stop at any time if it becomes too overwhelming.

You can't know how many sessions will be required until you start the process. If you are dealing with a single traumatic event, you may only need a few sessions. If your PTSD is the result of ongoing trauma, it could take a lot longer for your brain to build the new neural pathways needed to heal. However long it takes, the research shows that the results are long lasting, with the effects still present over a year after the end of a 12-session program***1.

## Side Effects

The side effects of EMDR vary between individuals. You may find yourself having vivid dreams or experiencing a heightened sense of awareness in the wake of a session. You may also find yourself feeling emotional, which is perfectly normal and something you can discuss with your therapist.

The most important thing is that you're kind to yourself during this process. You might like to schedule something soothing after sessions to help you assimilate what came up, like a walk, swim, or massage. Your brain is so used to living in a state of trauma that it will want to stay in its old habits. This can mean that your distress levels will increase before they lessen, so it's important to be open with your therapist about how you're feeling so they can go at a pace that won't retraumatize you.

However, while EMDR has a high success rate, it isn't universal. For some people, while it brings up the trauma, it doesn't always process, so you're put in a state where you're reliving your experiences with nowhere for that trauma to go. If you think this may be your experience, you should talk about it with your therapist. Other therapies are available and while some discomfort is normal - and a sign of healing - you shouldn't be left feeling worse.

## IFS (INTERNAL FAMILY SYSTEMS) THERAPY

*Leigh's story:*

*I first heard of IFS on an online trauma discussion group. I'd tried talk therapy in the past but had found it didn't help. I'd been self-medicating with alcohol instead, but I knew that this wasn't a long-term solution. I was harming myself even more than I'd already been. My drinking was pushing away the people I loved and I knew I had to stop.*

*I was intrigued by the idea that IFS would help me identify those aspects of myself that were acting out to protect the parts damaged by trauma. Drinking had made me feel lost and alone. Working with my IFS therapist, I was able to figure out what I needed and how I could face my trauma and heal it instead of burying it under booze.*

### What To Expect From IFS Therapy

IFS therapy is based on the notion that everyone is an ecosystem composed of a core self surrounded by various different parts. When there is an imbalance in this ecosystem, some of these parts can behave in self-destructive or disturbing behaviors as a means to protect damaged and vulnerable parts. While it is believed that all those different parts want the best for the core self, they do not always have healthy ways available to support the core self.

As an example, let's say you have a part of yourself that always feels anxious in social situations. In IFS therapy, you would first identify and acknowledge that anxious part. You would give it your full attention and let it express itself. You might discover that this part developed because it wants to protect you from potential rejection or embarrassment.

Next, you would explore how other parts of yourself feel about this anxious part. Maybe there's another part that resents the anxious part because it believes it hinders your confidence. You would work on understanding and addressing the concerns of these different parts.

As you continue the therapy, you would start fostering a dialogue between these parts and your core self. You would build trust and reassure the anxious part that its intentions are valued. This process helps the parts of yourself come together and communicate effectively.

In the final stage, you would ask the anxious part about its fears. It might be afraid that if it lets go of its protective role, you will face rejection or harm. By addressing these fears and working through the underlying issues, your core self becomes stronger and more capable of handling social situations without excessive anxiety.

This is just a simplified example, but it illustrates how IFS therapy helps you understand and heal different parts of yourself, fostering internal harmony and healthier coping strategies. An IFS therapist works with you to locate all your different parts, discover what they need and fulfill their needs so they can rebalance.

There are six steps or Fs to IFS therapy:

1. **Find.** Initially you will be guided to discover which parts of your self need attention. At this stage, you are not looking to fix anything, merely understand what these parts are telling you. They could be communicating through thoughts, feelings, or physical sensations. You may talk about your observations with your therapist or simply be supported to sit with them and allow the aspects of your being to step forward as needed.

2. **Focus.** After you've identified a part that needs help, you turn your full attention to it. Allow it to carry out whatever behaviors it needs and give it room to be. During this stage, you are letting it know that it has your focus. Often, these parts act out because they have an unmet need. Enabling them to feel seen and heard encourages a more authentic expression.

3. **Flesh out.** Once you've given a part your full attention, it will become a group of physical feelings and emotions. You may find that you receive signals from this part. Be open to hearing what it has to say to you or what memories it brings up.

   The first three steps may take a while to work if you haven't had IFS before or you may move through them quickly if you're familiar with IFS. Be open to allowing your experience to be what you experience. It takes as long as it takes and there is no pressure to conform to a specific timetable.

4. **Feel toward.** Having worked with one part of yourself, you will then deal with the other parts to see how they feel about this part. It may be that other parts of yourself resent it getting so much attention or have concerns that giving it your focus could lead to even more imbalance. This is the time to assess whether your core self is strong enough to hold all these parts together. If not, you may need to work with these other parts to smooth the way before you can progress. This strength is measured through the eight Cs of calm, compassion, curiosity, clarity, confidence, courage, creativity, and connection. If you feel any of these while working with the part under focus, you have the strength to nurture it. If not, or there are other more negative emotions such as rage or worry, this means that there is another part in play trying to cope with the part in question.

5. **Befriend.** Up until this point you will have been working with parts of yourself as separate entities. Now it's time to start bringing these together to foster communication between the parts and your core self. There needs to be trust between the part and your self, so now you open up a dialog with the part to find out what it wants to achieve, how it thinks it's helping, and reassure it that its contribution is important and valued.

6. **Fear.** In this final stage, we ask the part about its fears. Up until now it's been trying to protect you. What does it think might happen if it lets go of that role? It may well be that

at this stage you will see things come up that have been kept locked up tightly in the past so they wouldn't hurt you. If you've worked effectively through all the previous steps, your core self will be able to support the part to move away and allow the self to deal with whatever the part has been protecting.

IFS looks different for everyone. While there is a framework to follow, you will work through it in your own time in a way that works best for you. Ultimately, the most important thing is that you learn to be kind and compassionate to all aspects of yourself and are able to feel safe throughout this process. I had some incredible moments of healing with IFS, especially when I combined it with EMDR. Getting in touch with my inner child has been incredibly therapeutic for me in letting go of some of the negative belief systems I was holding on to.

## Negative aspects of IFS therapy

As with all therapies, IFS isn't right for everyone and it's important you find a therapist who is appropriately qualified and who makes you feel comfortable. Since the process involves dealing with yourself as separate entities, each tasked with a specific role, it can be difficult to fully appreciate the precise cause of your trauma and the underlying issues when there can be multiple parts at play trying to prevent this trauma from resurfacing.

If you attempt to reintegrate parts of your self before they are ready, this can make your issues worse because they'll go into overdrive to try and protect you even more, which can cause further damage. Your therapist needs to understand **all** of your parts to support you to work effectively and establish more positive coping strategies than your current ones. If you've suffered extreme trauma, you may have developed extraneous parts to deal with it that make it difficult to go deeper into the underlying parts. Clearing these unnecessary parts out of the way can be a difficult experience and you may need to utilize other therapies such as EMDR to work on them.

## GESTALT THERAPY

*Zach's story:*

*I was brought up in a very strict household. We were taught not to complain about the past. My dad always used to say "I don't want to hear about it. What's done is done." A strict disciplinarian, he wasn't averse to using physical punishment to keep his kids in line.*

*When I decided to seek therapy for my abusive childhood, I struggled to open up about the past. Those lessons that were beaten into me were hard to move past.*

*Seeing my struggle with reliving my history, my therapist suggested we try Gestalt therapy. I found that focusing on the present and leaving my childhood firmly in the past was much better for me. Reliving my trauma only made me feel worse, but focusing on the present moment helped me break free of my past. Now I'm in conscious control of my thoughts and I get to choose whether to allow my childhood to affect me.*

Not everyone wants to relive their trauma. While many therapies involve confronting your experiences to process them, Gestalt therapy takes a different approach. It keeps the focus on the present moment, supporting the patient to develop self-awareness and emotional awareness that supports them moving forward.

## What To Expect From Gestalt Therapy

Gestalt therapy is a holistic, client centered form of psychotherapy that supports the patient to look for current issues in their lives that reflect their life challenges without the need to dig deep into their past. It places your experiences in context and explores how you can take responsibility for your choices when dealing with a situation. It helps you understand how you are influenced by your subjective thoughts and ways of being as much as external events.

A Gestalt therapist will hold space for you to explore what's true for you without judgment. They will support you to become more aware of your experiences, perceptions, and responses to current events. They take the approach that as you become increasingly self-aware, you will naturally overcome the ways in which you're holding yourself back. The process takes as long as it takes. You aren't forced, hurried or pressured to come to specific conclusions. Difficult memories will come up only when you're ready to heal from them. The idea is that you figure things out in a way that makes sense for you.

Since Gestalt therapy is unusual among trauma therapies in that it keeps the focus on the present, your therapist will help keep you in the here and now if they feel you're spending too much time dwelling on the past or worrying about the future. So, for example, you might be asked about your facial expression or body language while you're processing a specific event. In being asked about what's happening in the present, you're supported to be mindful of what's currently going on rather than allowing the past to rule your thoughts.

You also may be taken through role play, guided imagery, or the use of props to nurture understanding. It's an experience that's unique to the individual because you're the one in control.

### Side Effects Of Gestalt Therapy

Not everyone finds Gestalt therapy helpful. The lack of a formal structure can be difficult for those who prefer to know what to expect and need a sense of control to cope with their trauma. If you feel that you need to explore your trauma in order to resolve it, you may find it frustrating to be guided to keep your focus on the present. You may not enjoy your therapist observing your body language and emotions. Some people report that some of the techniques feel forced and unnatural, such as pretending someone is sitting in an empty chair in front of you so you can talk with them about an event.

If you or your Gestalt therapist feel that you've gone as far as you can using the techniques, you can ask to be referred to a different therapist offering a different modality.

## COGNITIVE BEHAVIORAL THERAPY (CBT)

*Jayne's story:*

*I developed PTSD after serving in Afghanistan. There was one particular incident that stuck in my mind. I saw some of my fellow service members die when their combat supply truck was hit by an IED [improvised explosive device]. With the help of my therapist, I decided to try CBT to deal with the ongoing effects of trauma.*

*First I was given cognitive worksheets so I could start noting down significant events, my thoughts about those events and how they made me feel. It was eye opening seeing the thoughts that came up whenever I remembered what had happened in Afghanistan. One thought I had was, "It was my fault they died. I should have told them to wait until we knew the way ahead was clear." The associated feeling was guilt.*

*I took my worksheets to my next therapy session. My therapist took me through what she called 'Socratic dialog' to work through this thought. She helped me see that I had followed the correct procedure before the explosion. There were no signs of danger and if the people in the truck hadn't spotted the threat, I didn't stand a chance of seeing it to warn them. She also supported me to recognize that if I hadn't followed protocols, it's possible something even worse could have happened.*

*I was able to reframe my thought to "I correctly followed protocol in a challenging situation and may have stopped something worse happening." I was able to feel less guilty, especially since I realized that my friend who died probably would have done exactly the same thing in my situation.*

*CBT definitely eased my trauma symptoms.*

CBT is one of the most commonly used forms of therapy to treat a wide range of mental health problems including PTSD. It focuses on the connection between thoughts, feelings, and behaviors and how changes in any one of those areas can improve function in the other areas. It deals with current problems and symptoms and is usually given in 12-16 sessions in either an individual or group format.

## What To Expect From CBT Sessions

Emotional processing theory[2] posits that when you go through a traumatic event, you can develop negative associations with reminders of the event that aren't traumatic, such as news stories, situations, and people. This can lead to erroneous thoughts, such as "I am always under threat" and emotional reactions like fear or feeling numb. Changing these associations is at the core of CBT.

Therapists use a range of techniques such as cognitive restructuring, journaling and thought records, role play, and relaxation/stress reduction techniques, to reduce trauma symptoms and improve cognitive function. You are likely to be guided to re-evaluate the way you think and the assumptions you've made about yourself as a consequence of your trauma to identify unhelpful thought patterns like pessimism, negative thought patterns, and assuming the worst to encourage a more balanced, effective way of thinking. This helps you to reframe your understanding of your experiences as well as the way you see yourself and your ability to deal with your trauma.

You will work collaboratively with your therapist to decide on a treatment plan. You are likely to learn more about trauma and its impact on you as you progress, as well as learn stress management techniques and plan for how to cope when something triggering happens. The ultimate aim is to give you back a sense of control and self-confidence to reduce or eliminate more negative coping mechanisms.

## The Negative Aspects Of CBT

Not everyone finds CBT useful. You will need to fully commit and engage in the process in order to benefit from it and not everyone is ready/capable of doing that. Doing the extra assignments in between therapy sessions can take up a lot of time and it may not be suitable if you have more complex mental health needs or have learning difficulties.

You'll need to face difficult emotions and your anxieties head on. This may make you feel worse, at least in the short term. CBT also won't delve into any other underlying problems in systems or families that could be affecting your health and wellbeing. Critics of CBT have argued that although it tackles the problems you're currently facing and deals with specific issues, it doesn't deal with underlying causes, such as trauma, so may not offer a complete solution.

## COGNITIVE PROCESSING THERAPY (CPT)

*Anton's story:*

*When I was 17 my best friend killed himself. I had no idea that he was feeling like that and for years I beat myself up for not seeing the signs or being able to help him.*

*When I went to college, I was in a film studies lecture. The lecturer was playing music that had shaped the mood of movies. Gangsta's Paradise by Coolio came on and suddenly I was in floods of tears.*

*My college had really good student support, so they arranged for me to see a counselor. They told me that I was suffering from PTSD and therapy could help. I was advised to try cognitive processing therapy to help me deal with the loss of my friend. At first it was hard to think about what had happened to him, but as I worked through therapy, I was able to see that his death wasn't my fault. CPT helped me realize that the best way to honor him was to remember our good times together and not to blame myself for what happened.*

CPT is a specific type of cognitive behavioral therapy that is known to be effective in dealing with the symptoms of PTSD.[3] It is generally delivered over 12 sessions, either 1:1 or in a group format. It helps you to identify and change unhelpful beliefs connected to your trauma, enabling you to reframe traumatic events to limit their impact on your life.

## What To Expect From CPT Sessions

Trauma can change how you view yourself and the world around you. You may blame yourself for your experiences or decide the world is threatening and scary. These thoughts can keep you trapped in trauma and negatively impact your enjoyment of life. CPT teaches you skills to change how you view your trauma. You become adept at examining whether there are facts that support your thoughts or if they're just thoughts. You can then decide whether you want to change those thoughts.

In your first session you'll cover what will happen during your treatment. Your therapist will give you information about PTSD so you can understand your symptoms. You may be asked about the nature of your trauma but at this stage you won't need to explore it in great detail. You will then be tasked with doing some writing about the impact of your trauma.

In subsequent sessions, you'll discuss any negative or unhelpful thoughts that have come up around your trauma and you'll work with your therapist to explore other ways of thinking about the situation. You'll be given worksheets to use during sessions and at home to reinforce your new ways of thinking.

After a few sessions, you may be asked to write about your trauma in detail. This is so you can handle strong emotions like anger, sadness and guilt by talking through the situation with your therapist.

Towards the end of your course of therapy, your therapist will help you explore specific areas that may have been impacted by trauma such as your sense of safety, trust, or control, self-esteem, and intimacy.

## The Risks Of CPT

For most people, CPT is a highly effective therapy. Side effects are rare and generally tend to be confined to mild to moderate distress when dealing with trauma-related memories or beliefs. These usually pass quickly and people feel better as they progress through therapy.

The majority of people who go through CPT find that the benefits are worth any passing discomfort and the effects are long lasting.[4]

## PROLONGED EXPOSURE

*Becky's story:*

*In 2004, I was on a trip of a lifetime spending Christmas in Thailand. I had no idea that this would end up with me surviving the deadliest tsunami in recent times.*

*I'd hired a minivan and was touring the country. I was staying near the ocean. The views were spectacular.*

*But then the earthquake hit. I didn't know what to do. I figured I was best staying close to my minivan in case I needed to get away. But then I heard a loud noise unlike anything I'd ever heard. I looked out to see and saw something I'd never seen before. I was petrified.*

*I ran into my minivan, my hands shaking as I tried to get my key into the ignition. The black wave hit my minivan, rolling it over several times before I lost consciousness.*

*When I woke up, I was floating in dirty water. I grabbed onto a log and clung to it as I floated through bodies and debris. I had no idea where I was when eventually I washed ashore. I was starving and thirsty.*

*I took shade under a mangrove tree and started foraging for anything I could find to eat or drink. I managed to salvage some bottles of water and a few packs of noodles, but I soon went through them.*

*Somehow I survived for almost three weeks before I was rescued by people who'd come to recover the bodies. I was taken to Fakinah hospital which is where I found out just how bad the disaster had been.*

*I know I'm blessed to have survived, but for years I struggled with PTSD. I avoided anything to do with the ocean. I couldn't watch films or TV shows that featured beaches. I even moved to Colorado to be as far away from the sea as possible. I hated being alone with my thoughts, so I spent as much time at work as I could and then signed up for countless hobbies and classes so I never had time to think about what had happened to me.*

*Colleagues would tell me they admired my work ethic and wondered how I managed to do it all. They had no idea what was really going on with my mind. But the harder I worked to avoid thinking about the tsunami, the more intrusive those thoughts became. I couldn't hold down a relationship because my nightmares were too disturbing for anyone to witness.*

*It was a particularly nasty breakup that caused me to seek treatment. I knew the things my ex accused me of weren't true. I wasn't crazy. I'd just been through something most people couldn't even imagine.*

*After I was diagnosed with PTSD and discussing my symptoms, it was decided that the best treatment for me was exposure therapy alongside CBT. My therapist guided me to give him a detailed account of my experiences during the tsunami. We did this again and again, each time, my therapist asking for more and more details to help me regain control of my anxiety.*

*These sessions were recorded so I could listen to them outside of therapy.*

*With the support of my therapist, I finally faced my fears and my symptoms reduced the more I was exposed to my memories. I was able to recognize that even though I might feel fear and anxiety while talking about the tsunami, these were just feelings and they would always pass. Over time, I was able to feel comfortable telling people about what I'd been through. I managed to book a beach holiday and relax in the sun. I was no longer afraid of being alone with my memories. I know now that it's just a thought. It can't harm me.*

Prolonged exposure helps trauma sufferers to learn how to deal with their memories, feelings and situations. It supports patients to put them into context and understand that they're not a threat and don't have to be avoided.

## What To Expect From Prolonged Exposure

Prolonged exposure is a strategy that can be used in CBT to help individuals tackle the fear associated with traumatic events. It's a natural instinct to want to avoid anything that's a reminder of the trauma, but this avoidance only increases the fear. By facing up to those memories instead, PTSD symptoms can be reduced because the individual learns that anything related to the trauma isn't dangerous in and of itself so doesn't need to be avoided.

Prolonged exposure usually takes place over around three months of weekly sessions of 60-120 minutes. In an initial assessment you'll be given an overview of treatment and your therapist will gain a greater understanding of the experiences that have brought you to this point. You are also likely to be given breathing techniques to cope with anxiety.

After this first assessment, exposure begins. Since it can be a very anxiety-inducing experience, your therapist will work hard to create a safe space for you to deal with your fears. You will be supported through imaginal and in vivo exposure at a pace that suits you.

**Imaginal exposure** takes place in sessions with your therapist. You will describe the event as if it's happening right now. You'll then discuss and process any emotions that have come up for you. These descriptions will be recorded so you can listen to them between sessions to continue processing the emotions and practice breathing through your anxiety.

**In vivo exposure** is homework you're given to face up to associated stimuli outside of therapy. You'll work with your therapist to put together a list of possible triggers associated with your trauma and then agree on which ones you'll face in between sessions. You'll be encouraged to push yourself but in incremental steps so you can experience success when faced with triggers and dealing with the ensuing emotion.

## Side Effects Of Prolonged Exposure

While the US Department of Veteran Affairs describes prolonged exposure as the "gold standard" of PTSD treatment, it is a controversial therapy. Many people find that it makes their trauma symptoms much worse. It has made many veterans violent, depressed or even suicidal. It has an estimated drop out rate of over 50%, far higher than other forms of therapy.[5]

As such, you should proceed with prolonged exposure with caution and only after discussing with your therapist whether it really is the best approach for you.

## Narrative Exposure Therapy

*Simon's story:*

*When I was 18, I was a victim of a home invasion. My parents, sister and I were all tied up while three men ransacked our house. Although the gang were caught and convicted, I couldn't stop obsessing over the possibility of it happening again. I had recurrent nightmares and flashbacks. I avoided being in any situation that made me feel out of control. I always had to be the one driving anywhere - I couldn't cope sitting in the passenger seat.*

*It took ten years for me to seek treatment. I happened to be dating a woman who was a psychiatric nurse and she helped me see that what I was experiencing wasn't normal. I guess I'd always known on some level, but my trauma response was keeping me safe. I didn't want to lower my guard in case something bad happened.*

*I started seeing a therapist and they suggested I try narrative exposure therapy. Over six 90-minute sessions we wrote out a description of my life so far. It included some of my happiest childhood memories, but when it came to writing about the attack my thoughts were fragmented, filled with intrusive memories of the smell of fear, the sound of my mom and sister crying, the feeling of my hands being tied together.*

*My therapist helped me face up to those feelings and sensations, put them into a coherent form and include them in the narrative. Once we'd finished, my therapist helped me explore other challenging events until we'd processed them all up to the present day. I was presented with a print out of my story. I still read it sometimes.*

*While I still felt a little nervous about the possibility of another home invasion, for the first time I could talk about what had happened to me without panicking. At a six month follow up session, my symptoms had reduced so much I no longer met the criteria for having Complex PTSD.*

Narrative exposure therapy is thought of as being particularly useful for individuals suffering from Complex PTSD. It is most often offered in group sessions who receive between four to ten sessions although it can also be offered individually. It is based on the premise that the stories we tell ourselves about our lives influence how we interpret our experiences. When we define our stories solely through the lens of trauma, we experience ongoing trauma and distress.

## What To Expect From Narrative Exposure Therapy

With the support of a trained professional, you put together a chronological narrative of your life focusing mainly on traumatic experiences but also including some positive events to put your trauma into context. By redefining your life story in a coherent fashion, you are able to understand that trauma does not have to define you.

You will be asked to describe your emotions, thoughts, sensory experiences and physiological responses in great detail. You'll be helped to relive your trauma while staying connected to the present so you can process your responses. At the end of your course of therapy, you'll be given a copy of your autobiography to keep.

When recounting your entire life story, you don't need to focus on any one specific traumatic event. Instead, you can consider your whole life which helps you to recognize and adjust behavioral patterns and schemas you've created over the years.

Narrative exposure therapy takes a different approach to other treatments because it focuses on putting together the story of what happened in a fashion that helps you regain your self-respect and recognizes your human rights. For many patients, knowing that you'll get a written biography when you conclude your treatment is a strong motivation for sticking with the program.

## The Risks Of Narrative Exposure Therapy

As with all forms of trauma therapy, not everyone will be suited to narrative exposure therapy. Some may struggle to remember what they experienced and find it retraumatizing to try. However, evidence would suggest that for most trauma sufferers who complete treatment, this is an effective form of therapy.[6]

## PSYCHEDELIC-ASSISTED THERAPIES

*Eric's story:*

*My time in Iraq shaped who I am today - and for a long time, I didn't like who that was. I spent most of my adult life dealing with recurrent nightmares, intrusive thoughts and survivor's guilt. I lived alone, shunning the company of others as much as possible. I spent my days thinking about all the mistakes I'd made and what I should have done instead.*

*I knew my parents were worried about me, but I shrugged off their concerns for years. Eventually, I got sick of their nagging and agreed to try psychotherapy. Man, that was a mistake! I became so overwhelmed by panic attacks that I had to quit. I'd rather be back in Iraq than on that therapist's couch.*

*But then I heard about an MDMA assisted therapy session through one of my veteran's support groups. I'd read about how psychedelics could help with trauma, but I wasn't sure it would work on me. Still, I figured it couldn't get any worse than the mess I was currently in.*

*When I took MDMA, I was in a heightened state of consciousness, yet I felt perfectly safe. I was in a state of blissful calm I don't think I'd ever experienced in my life. As my therapist guided me to talk through what had happened to me, I didn't get the same anxiety I had in the past. It was like I was talking about things that had happened to someone else.*

*I was able to realize that I'd only done what I had to do to survive. The people I fought were only doing what they thought was best. They just wanted to live too. I felt connected to everyone in the world in a way that was pure, empathetic and filled with love.*

*After that single MDMA session I was referred to traditional psychotherapy. This time it was different and I was able to finally get relief from my trauma symptoms.*

Plants with psychedelic properties have been used in herbal medicine for centuries to promote healing. Recent studies have found that these psychedelics can have a positive effect on mental illness such as depression or anxiety as well as reducing the impact of trauma.[7]

## What To Expect From Psychedelic-Assisted Therapies

Under the supervision of an appropriately qualified professional, you will take a dose of a psychedelic medicine which may have been derived from a plant or created in a lab. The most commonly used psychedelics are psilocybin (so-called magic mushrooms), LSD, ketamine, ayahuasca and MDMA.

While under the influence of the drug, you will experience an altered state of consciousness. This may include hallucinations, a change in perception of sensation or shifts in your sense of space and time. You might also experience a profound sense of inner peace, loving kindness towards yourself and others and even spiritual breakthroughs.

When this is combined with psychotherapy, it can generate healing on a deeper level than therapy alone. This is believed to be because psychedelics enable you to explore traumatic experiences from a different perspective. Since the drugs can make you feel safe and loved and give you a sense of meaning or purpose, this makes it easier to process trauma. In one study, 88% of participants with severe PTSD reported a major reduction in their symptoms with 67% considered to be fully recovered just two months after treatment.[8]

## The Risks Of Psychedelic-Assisted Therapy

While there is increasing evidence to show how incredible psychedelics can be in the treatment of PTSD, there is still a lot of stigma attached to taking these kinds of drugs. Since psychedelics are illegal in the United States and many other countries, patients are often forced to travel to other countries or rely on word of mouth to find therapists willing to offer these drugs illegally.

As with all drugs, there's always a risk of side effects. For some people, psychedelics can make their symptoms worse. As such, you should always take them under the supervision of an appropriately qualified professional.

However, the Food and Drug Administration has given approval for some psychedelic medicines to be researched providing this was to the same standard as conventional medicine. This has led to many studies showing how effective these drugs are and there is a possibility they will be approved for therapeutic use in the future.

## SOMATIC THERAPY

*Liz's story:*

*I'd been through a lot of therapy which had helped me come to terms with an abusive childhood. I had a strong understanding of who I was and what I wanted. But I was still suffering from the impact of trauma. I was self-aware enough to recognize when it was the trauma speaking rather than me, but I seemed to have hit a wall in terms of breaking through to the next level. I was done with talking about my childhood. I felt all talked out. I couldn't see how even more talking was going to help.*

*I came across an article about somatic healing and it seemed to be the missing puzzle piece. I did some more research and I really thought it was what I needed to finally leave the past behind. My mind and body needed to understand that I was safe and know how that felt. I'd been living in a state of fight or flight for so long it had become my normal state of being. I hoped somatic healing would help my physical body learn a different way.*

*I was surprised at how simple the techniques were at my first session. We did some mind-body work where I was guided through some breathwork exercises and we finished with a massage. Bliss! On the surface it was hard to make the mental connection between what we were doing and healing trauma, but that was part of the point. I'd spent too long living in my mind and needed to feel grounded in my body.*

*After just one session I already felt less stressed. Over the following weeks we worked on releasing stress and trauma on my body. Although we did talk a little about how I was feeling, our focus was very much on my physical experiences rather than my emotional wellbeing. I had no idea the two were so closely connected, but the somatic healing sessions showed me how important it was to look after my whole self and not just a part of me.*

*I'm a different person now. I've finally healed the wounds of my childhood and I can look forward to a future where I'm free to do whatever I want without worrying about triggering my trauma.*

Somatic therapy treats PTSD through the mind-body connection. This more physical approach to trauma helps release stress and tension that becomes trapped in the body following traumatic experiences to promote mental healing.

## What To Expect From A Somatic Therapy Session

Somatic therapists have a range of tools available and sessions will vary according to the needs of the individual. One of the most common methods involves talking about your problems as you would in other types of therapy. However, the difference here is that you will be guided to focus on what you're feeling in your body as you discuss your trauma. Based on your responses, you'll then be taken through mind-body exercises such as breath work, meditation, visualization, massage, or dance.

Somatic therapy is a genuinely holistic approach that works with the whole self. It is based in the theory that it's not just your mind that remembers trauma, but your body does as well. As you work through somatic therapy, you'll develop a greater awareness of your body and the messages it sends you. You'll be given tools to help you calm yourself when you're feeling stressed or anxious and ways of releasing tension in the body to still the mind. You'll experience an emotional release and use movement to express physical feelings.

If you've found that talk therapy hasn't been effective for you or you simply don't want to try, somatic therapy offers a very different approach to healing your trauma. There is evidence to show that it's a highly effective treatment for PTSD, although more is needed to understand which specific patients will benefit the most from it.[9]

## The Risks Of Somatic Therapy

As with all trauma therapies, there are some risks associated with somatic therapy which means it's not right for everyone. You are working in close physical proximity with your therapist which may be retraumatizing for some, especially if you were physically or sexually abused. While this may be the result of misinterpreting your therapist's touch rather than deliberate abuse of power, the outcome is the same.

Another potential risk is what's known as inappropriate regression, which is when you regress without any therapeutic reason, which may build an infantile dependency between you and your therapist akin to a parent-child relationship.

As with any other treatment, choose your therapist with care and make sure they are appropriately qualified and accredited with a professional body.

# INNER CHILD WORK

*Sylvie's story:*

*My childhood wasn't exactly what you'd call idyllic. My parents split up when I was a baby. Apparently, my dad came back a few times to see me, but I don't remember because those visits stopped by the time I was two.*

*My mom went through a never ending stream of boyfriends. I never knew who would be sitting at the breakfast table the next morning. When I hit puberty, Mom started to see me as a threat to her 'relationships.' It didn't matter that none of them ever lasted more than a few weeks, she started to blame me for stealing her boyfriends. Like I would ever want to date the lowlifes she brought home.*

*I couldn't wait to leave home, but as an adult I always thought that I was overly sensitive. I struggled to express myself and felt like I was going to let my friends and colleagues down, even though I hadn't done anything wrong. I was working twice as hard as anyone else to make sure I didn't make mistakes and it was exhausting.*

*I had a nervous breakdown in my mid-twenties. This forced me to seek therapy which is when I learned about my inner child. This is the part of your subconscious that never grew up. We all have one but for some of us - like me - our inner child is traumatized and remembers the emotions of a difficult childhood. When we're triggered, those emotions can come out and affect our thoughts and actions. This is why we find ourselves repeating patterns of behavior, even when they're negative.*

*My therapist worked with me to heal my inner child. Through journaling and guided visualizations, I connected with her and learned about the specific events that had led to my ultimate breakdown. I was able to offer her the healing and comfort I needed at the time. It might sound silly, but the more I dealt with my inner child, the more at peace I felt.*

*I'm no longer seeing my therapist but I still practice meditations to heal my inner child. I do things to delight and entertain her in my daily life as well! I play more - I do the things I enjoyed as a child but let go for reasons I can't even articulate. I eat ice cream right from the tub, spend hours coloring and I've even taken up roller skating!*

*I'm so much happier now my inner child has the affection and nurturing she's always needed.*

If you've experienced trauma as a child, your inner child will bury those experiences and the associated emotion as a survival instinct. We are helpless as children. We have no choice but to live with and depend upon our caregivers. If those caregivers neglect or harm us, it has an incredibly damaging effect on our emotions. In order to protect ourselves, our inner children hide those feelings of rejection, fear, worthlessness and shame.

Unfortunately, the unintended side effect of this self-protection strategy is that these children grow up into adults who are trapped in patterns of self-sabotage. You may struggle to build meaningful connections or achieve your goals, even if you really want something. You may look to your partner to fulfill the role of parent and then be hurt when they can't live up to your expectations.

Alternatively, you may avoid relationships completely so no one can ever hurt you again.

## What To Expect From Inner Child Work

While you do not need a therapist to do inner child work, when it comes to healing trauma, it's always a good idea to at least start with professional support. You may find that the memories and emotions that come up can be retraumatizing. Having a therapist hold space for you during this process will make it easier for you to cope with difficult emotions.

Not all emotions will be negative, however. Your inner child also has all the innocence, happiness and fearless confidence that was your birthright. It is just as likely that these emotions will come up for you at times during the healing process.

A traumatic childhood makes it hard to move on as an adult. However, the effects will linger unless you actively do something to release their hold on you. It can be painful to dig up those (probably) long forgotten memories, but once you've worked through them you can finally heal from your past. The really cool part is that when you heal your inner child, you don't just release negative emotions. You'll discover all those gifts that have been hidden for so long. Your relationships improve, you'll no longer feel the need to follow negative patterns of behavior to cope with your trauma and you develop a stronger sense of who you are and what you truly want.

There are various exercises your therapist might give you to connect with your inner child. You might connect with your inner child and discuss the various stages of your childhood and how you felt each step of the way. You could write a letter to your inner child to tell them how much you love and respect them. Reassure them that they are safe and they can trust you. Then you might have your inner child write a letter back to you. You might do an inner child visualization to talk to your inner child face-to-face and discuss what they need from you to heal their pain.

You may be encouraged to keep an inner child work journal. As you explore your inner turmoil, recording it will help you process your experiences even further. In addition, it will be a record of your progress and show how far you've come, encouraging you to keep going.

## The Problems With Inner Child Work

Inner child work is highly eclectic and utilized by therapists with a background in various modalities. However, research on its effectiveness is scant, with most of it relying on individual case studies rather than larger scale controlled studies. There's more evidence to support the use of inner child work in conjunction with other therapies, but this then makes it difficult to say with any real certainty what the specific impact of inner child healing might be.

Also, if you choose to do inner child work independently, you risk pulling up more trauma without professional support to cope with it.

# ENERGY WORK

*Jo's story:*

*I'd always been open to alternative healing methods. I'm a Reiki II myself, so I know first hand how miraculous energy work can be.*

*After a traumatic birth experience with my second child, I decided to work with an energy healer to help me cope with what had happened. I should say that I was also seeing a more traditional therapist, but I felt that just talking about my daughter's birth wasn't going to be enough to heal my trauma. I was struggling to bond with my daughter the way I had with my son and I was sliding into postnatal depression. I was determined to be the best mother I could be, so I knew I needed help to be her.*

*Everything is energy. That's a simple scientific fact. So it stood to reason that if I could get my energies back into alignment, then a lot of the problems I was experiencing as a result of my trauma would resolve themselves naturally.*

*I regularly gave myself reiki to help ease the symptoms of birth trauma. My energy healer also supported my work with EFT (emotional freedom therapy) as well as giving me energy healing both during our sessions and from a distance.*

*I have no doubt that the energy work I did was the reason why I had such a strong response to the CBT work I was doing with my therapist. Now my daughter and I have a very strong bond and I don't find myself reliving the details of her birth every time I look at her. My husband and I are even talking about having another baby.*

Energy healing is based on the notion that when we go through trauma, it disrupts our energy. It becomes frozen or blocked, affecting our daily functioning and general health. By restoring balance to our energy, we will by default experience an improvement in our trauma symptoms.

## What To Expect From An Energy Healing Session

There are various energy modalities available to help with your trauma. As such, you will need to speak to your energy healer to discover what a typical session will look like. As a general rule, you will generally take a passive role in the process. Your job is to allow the healing facilitated by your energy practitioner.

There are some forms such as EFT (emotional freedom therapy) which require a more active role in your part. EFT involves you tapping on various acupressure points on the body while talking about how your trauma makes you feel and then moving on to how you will feel once you're healed. There is evidence to suggest that the overwhelming majority of patients who practice EFT will experience a major reduction in symptoms in just a few sessions. What's more, these improvements are permanent.[10]

Reiki or 'life energy' is one of the better known forms of energy healing. It has been used by some mainstream medical organizations for its proven benefits.[11] Reiki can be given in-person or from a distance. If you are having an in-person session, you will remain fully clothed while you sit or lie down. All you need to do is relax as the Reiki practitioner places their hands on or above different parts of the body for a few minutes at each point until the energy has had a chance to do its work.

Reiki helps release blocked or trapped energy by putting the body and mind into deep relaxation, allowing you to free hidden emotions so you can process them. It is generally used as a complementary therapy in conjunction with other clinically proven treatments. It may help take the edge off more traditional therapies, helping you avoid being retraumatized.

## The Problems With Energy Work

Scientific evidence is still lacking for many forms of energy work, so it may be that the placebo effect is more in play here than any real therapy. (Although there are some who would argue that it doesn't matter if it's a placebo - if it works, it works!)

There are many different forms of energy work available, some more plausible than others, and it is always possible that you might deal with a therapist who isn't what they say they are. If you can, work with someone you find through personal recommendations. If this isn't possible, ask any potential healer how they gained their skills and what experience they have with treating trauma patients. You should also check to see if they are insured in case of any problems.

There you have it. Eleven very different forms of therapy that may all help you heal from your trauma. Which one(s) you choose will depend on what's available in your area (although the internet has opened up more options since many therapists will now treat clients online) as well as what appeals to you.

Choose your therapist with care. You will be at your most vulnerable while working with them so it's important you feel you can trust them. It's okay to decide against working with a therapist, no matter how great their reputation, if you simply don't feel a connection with them. The most important thing is that you feel safe while you're with them.

In the next and final chapter, we're going to look at the lifestyle changes you can make to support your therapy and make sure your recovery is permanent. Let's move on from trauma once and for all!

# PART 4

## Lifestyle Practices

In this final part of the book, we're going to get seriously practical. I'm going to talk you through the changes you can make in your life right now to make a significant shift in your relationship with traumatic past events.

It is my aim that once you experience for yourself the positive impact these practices can make you'll be inspired to incorporate them into your routine for the rest of your life. Living without trauma really is a lifestyle not just a healing process. But I'm confident that once you see for yourself just how good life can be, you won't want to quit.

# 11

## YOUR TRAUMA-FREE LIFE

### Eleven Ways You Can Change Your Life To Overcome Trauma

*The best thing about a lot of these tools is that they are free. Breathwork, cold showers, walking, reading, meditating are there for you 24 hours a day. You just need to make time for them.*

## MY (GREG'S) STORY:

When I started working with Anna, some of her suggestions felt like they would be pointless for someone like myself. Being diagnosed with OCD, I couldn't sit still for 5 seconds so how the hell was I going to meditate for 30 minutes??

But as we made incremental changes to my daily routine, I noticed how these small habits began to stack up. I was going to therapy for an hour a week, but with the deep rooted trauma I'd suffered, an hour wasn't going to be nearly enough. I needed to be doing more. I guess that was the over achiever in me talking!

I knew that if I kept doing things the way I'd always done them, nothing was going to change. If I was serious about getting over my trauma, I needed to make some real changes in every aspect of my life.

Anna helped me implement my new way of living in incremental steps so it wasn't overwhelming. I think if I'd tried to make too many changes at once, none of them would have stuck. But making one small adjustment at a time and then allowing myself time to integrate this adjustment and to notice the positive effects made it easier for me to make another change, and then another.

I will always be grateful for Anna's help and the other therapists and healers who supported me on my journey. They directly inspired me to write this book to share what I learned so others could also realize that it *is* possible to live a life free from the grip of trauma. I had no idea life could be so good and I'm excited that you're going to learn how great it can be too!

If you're ready to do things differently, read on to discover a plethora of techniques that can help. You don't have to use all of them. Some of them will appeal more than others and you may find that some simply don't work for you and that's okay. Even incorporating one of these suggestions will reap dividends.

## EARLY MORNINGS

The thought of getting up any earlier than you already do may make you wince at the very notion, but there are a number of benefits to doing so. My life involved getting *home* from a club at 5am for 30 years. I don't *GET UP* at 5am!!! But greeting the day before anyone else you may be living with can be the best thing you ever do for yourself.

Waking up with the sun enables your body to wake up gradually and naturally instead of being jolted out of much-needed REM sleep by a piercing, sudden alarm. Your brain needs all the stages of sleep to learn, store memories, regulate your emotions - and process trauma. When you deprive yourself of your body's innate preference of waking slowly, you make it harder to achieve optimal health.

We think that staying up late means we can get more done, but we're usually exhausted by the evening and good for little more than flopping in front of the TV. Conversely, getting up early (and going to bed earlier) will give you essential quality time for yourself. If you're going through therapy, you may have homework that you can do first thing in the morning. Or, you might need to treat yourself to a little self care. Having time to savor your coffee while you read the early news or enjoying the stillness before the chaos of the day erupts can help you face whatever challenges may come.

Shifting your day to an earlier start can help you incorporate some of the other suggestions in this chapter. Working out and meditating before you get stuck into the daily grind will not only remove any temptation to skip a day because you've got too much on, it will also put you in a good mood thanks to all those feel-good endorphins released through exercise.

Since you're starting earlier, you might like to leave for work earlier and beat the rush hour. Research has shown that sitting in traffic may increase stress levels, depression, aggression and rage, none of which are good when you're suffering from trauma.[1]

One of the side effects of trauma is often sleep issues. Research has shown that those who wake up earlier usually go to bed earlier and have better quality sleep.[2] And better sleep means better moods, better concentration and more energy!

Have I convinced you yet? If so, you may want some help on how to become an early riser.

- **Gradually set your alarm fifteen minutes earlier.** Shift your start time every day for a week, slowly moving your waking time until you are getting up at the time you want. Don't make any exceptions for weekends either - this is a daily practice. At the same time, try going to bed fifteen minutes earlier so you don't wake up tired.

- **Find a way to motivate yourself.** Think of something you'll want to do that will bring you joy. What are you going to do with that extra hour or two? Do a morning meditation? Workout? Spend some time on a hobby? Bribery is also an option! You could go to your favorite coffee shop for a leisurely drink before you get stuck into the day.

- **Leave your bedroom.** Staying in bed after your alarm has gone off makes it more likely you'll fall asleep so you might end up being late or feeling sleepy. Once you're up, you're up!

- **Switch off screens early.** The blue light emitted by your devices is great for keeping you awake during the day, but avoiding it for the couple of hours before bed will help you relax and prepare for sleep.

- **Practice kindness to yourself.** Sometimes you will need to stay in bed for longer and that's okay. Maybe you're sick, were up late or simply have a nasty hangover. Allowing yourself the occasional lie in when you need will make it easier for you to be disciplined the rest of the time.

- **Don't eat heavy meals or spicy foods late at night.** This can cause heartburn or indigestion that can keep you awake, undoing all your hard work.

## ESTABLISH A MORNING ROUTINE

There's something truly magical about getting up before the sun and watching it rise. Many of the most successful people swear by their morning routines and with good reason. Once their day takes off, it's nothing but pressure and demands which can be overwhelming, especially if you're coping with trauma. A morning routine allows you to carry out the same basic tasks in the same order every day, which sets you up for whatever you've got to deal with.

How you spend those first few hours will affect the rest of the day. If you feel rushed from the moment you wake up, that feeling is likely to stick around. A morning routine, whatever it looks like, means you know you're getting off to a positive start, putting you in a good frame of mind, which will linger.

A morning routine will help you feel more productive. You know you're doing something useful from the moment you wake up. This sense of accomplishment will help you be better focused later in the day so you can complete all those tasks on your to-do list. Then at the end of the day, you'll feel confident that you did everything you could so you can relax and unwind without feeling like you should have done more.

Trauma sufferers are often dogged by a feeling that they lack control over their lives. If you've got a to-do list as long as your arm, your days can seem like a constant rush from one task to another. Your day controls you instead of the other way round, which negatively reinforces trauma symptoms. While a morning routine may only control the first few hours of your day, it's a step in the right direction of regaining control over the rest of your life.

A morning routine can help you avoid bad habits and replace them with healthy ones. You might use that extra time to eat a nutritious breakfast, practice meditation, exercise or even just make your bed. These healthy ways of being will carry over elsewhere in your life as you grow used to this new approach. You may find you naturally start eating better food, getting more exercise or spending less time looking for ways to numb the pain caused by your trauma.

## JOURNALING

There's something wonderfully therapeutic about journaling. It is increasingly being recommended by therapists because of its value in dealing with PTSD.[3] It can not only help with the symptoms of PTSD but also support you in post-traumatic growth, allowing you to find meaning in your experiences and making positive life changes as a result.

It's cheaper than a therapist too - all you need is a pen and paper, although you might like to splash out on a nice notebook for your journaling. You may even want more than one journal, such as one for gratitude and one for recording your thoughts and feelings.

The process is straightforward. Find a quiet time and place where you can sit with your thoughts and write about them. I highly recommend you do this with a pen and paper and not on your computer. Take a moment to consider how your PTSD or traumatic experiences have affected you then allow all those thoughts and feelings to flow onto the page without censoring yourself. Don't worry about spelling or grammar. This isn't a school assignment! The important thing is you get everything out on paper.

Try to make your writing as descriptive as possible. If you're feeling stressed after a particular event, record everything related to your feelings. What was going on in your body? Was your jaw clenched? Your shoulders tight? What were you thinking? This will help build your self-awareness. Beyond the stressful event, repeat the journaling process for at least two more days. This will help organize and shift the way you think and feel about the event.

If you can, try to write for at least 20 minutes, but if this isn't possible, don't worry. Some journaling is better than none. When you've finished writing, read over what you've written, noticing how you feel. Have your thoughts or feelings changed now you've written things out?

I think you'll be surprised at the impact of writing, being alone with your thoughts and expressing them to no one but the paper. I hope you'll be so surprised that you continue the process for life. A life worth living is a life worth recording.

## MEDITATION

Okay, you knew this was going to come up at some point. You may be sick of hearing people tell you meditation's all you need. You may have tried to meditate and found it impossible to maintain focus.

You may also have found that meditation makes your symptoms worse.

I want to caveat this suggestion with the fact that meditation isn't right for all people who have experienced trauma. Meditation involves sitting in stillness with your mind. Sometimes your mind can be a scary place to be! It can be triggering for some people to focus on their breath or adopt a particular posture for a certain amount of time.

If you are one of those people who finds that meditation increases your symptoms, leave it for a while and come back to it when you're further along your healing journey.

Now I've got the warnings out of the way, let's look at what meditation can do.

There are a lot of myths about what meditation should look like. It doesn't have to mean sitting in a cave chanting *Om* for three hours! Although if that's what you want to do, that could be an incredible experience.

The most common form of meditation is simply a sustained focus on a stimulus of your choosing. This could be your breath, a mantra, or an affirmation. There are plenty of guided meditations that are amazing at getting your brain to be still and focused.

Meditation does *not* mean emptying your mind of thoughts. Our brains are designed to think. That's what they do! So if you think you've failed at meditating because you couldn't clear your mind, you haven't. However, it might be that you haven't found the right technique for you. Not everyone gets on with all types of meditation and your preferences can change as you progress with your meditation practice.

There's a wealth of evidence to show that meditation can help with physical and mental health. It can improve heart health and lower blood pressure. It can reduce the symptoms associated with stress. It can help you get better sleep. The benefits of meditation are incalculable and are best experienced first hand to discover for yourself how life changing they can be.[4] There is less evidence concerning how meditation specifically helps with trauma but what is out there suggests that it can alleviate symptoms and support mental health.[5]

Here's a very simple meditation you can do to start your meditation practice.

Make yourself comfortable somewhere you won't be disturbed for a few minutes. You can sit or lie down, but I would advise sitting. We associate lying down with going to sleep. Meditation relaxes us so you may find yourself nodding off. While sleep is great and it may be you need more sleep, sleeping is not meditation. Break the association with relaxation and sleep by sitting up to meditate.

Close your eyes or allow your gaze to unfocus.

Turn your attention to your breath. Allow it to flow in and out without trying to control or change it in any way.

You might like to notice where you feel your breath in your body. Maybe you feel the air coming in and out of your nostrils. Maybe your attention is drawn to the rise and fall of your abdomen. Allow your experience to be unique, as you sit with your breath.

If you find that focusing on your breath makes you uncomfortable, you might like to open your eyes to focus on an object in the room instead. Observe it without judgment. Watch how the light falls, placing some parts in shadow.

As you sit with your breath or focus on the object you may find that thoughts or feelings arise without your wishing. When this happens, gently pull your attention back to your breath or the object.

There is nothing wrong with whatever you're thinking or feeling. Simply remind yourself that you do not need those thoughts or feelings right now and let them go so you can place your focus where you want it to be.

In this moment, you may be feeling relaxed or at peace. You may be feeling slight discomfort. You may be feeling nothing at all. However you feel is absolutely fine. Simply allow it to exist and know that this too will pass. Allow your experience be your experience, without judgment.

When you are ready, take a moment to feel gratitude for this experience, whatever it may have been.

Turn your attention to your body. How are you feeling now?

You might like to wriggle your fingers, wriggle your toes as you start to come back to the present moment. Perhaps you might want to stretch or even yawn.

When you are ready, open your eyes, if they have remained close..

There are numerous apps that have guided meditations. This is where I started. I think my first was 5 minutes long. As you get more familiar with the feeling, you'll get more confident to try for longer. Like anything we do, the more you do it, the easier it gets.

## MOVEMENT

Our bodies are designed to move. Yet so many of us live sedentary lifestyles that keep our bodies hunched over a keyboard, staring at a screen.

We know that exercise is good for us, but the word "exercise" generally comes with connotations of stress and misery. This is the opposite of what movement should be. Your body *thrives* on movement!

There are so many reasons why movement is good for us that go way beyond the obvious ones – weight loss and increased fitness. Moving your body is a known way of dealing with anxiety, stress and depression.[6]

Exercise also improves cognitive performance, which may have been impaired due to your trauma.[7] A healthy body supports a healthy mind, which means you'll feel good all over when you incorporate movement into your routine - literally!

If the thought of getting any exercise makes you think the only exercise you want is to run for the hills, relax. Movement doesn't have to mean running a marathon. It doesn't matter how you move, only that you do. Get active in whatever way suits your preferences. You're much more likely to stick with exercise if you choose a form that appeals to you. So, you could sign up for a high intensity spin class but you could just as easily go for a walk or get out in the garden.

Start looking for any opportunity you can to move your body. Can you walk instead of taking the car? Go up the stairs instead of taking the elevator? Get off the bus a stop earlier?

My back seems to be a constant source of aggravation. After 30 years of DJ'ing, a few accidents, and sports injuries, swimming seems to be one of the most beneficial forms of exercise for me. It's low impact and it uses just about every muscle in my body.

It's great for the cardiovascular system and really comes into its own in summer!

## YOGA

Having just discussed the merits of getting exercise, I want to take a moment to focus specifically on yoga. You may have heard some people dismiss it as 'just' stretching, but yoga is so much more. It is a holistic form of exercise that supports you to be in the moment, engaging the body to give the mind a rest. You'll find that when you do yoga, you'll be fully present in the moment and it's a moment that's full of peace and tranquility.

One aspect of yoga is to stretch the body and this can be an important tool to overcome trauma. We store so much mental tension in our fascia – the thin casing of connective tissue that surrounds and holds every organ, blood vessel, bone, nerve fiber and muscle in place It's a major part of our physical being and the primary source for storing our emotions.. When we stretch, we give ourselves the chance to release it. In addition, when we stretch, the body releases endorphins to make you feel good. It stimulates those receptors in the nervous system that slow down the production of stress hormones in the brain, naturally calming and soothing you.[8]

My favourite form is Yin Yoga, a slow paced discipline where the postures are held for 3-5 minutes, allowing the breath to naturally take us deeper into the stretches. This practice has often had me break out into tears or laughter as various emotions are released. And I always sleep like a baby afterwards!

The great thing about stretching is that it doesn't matter whether you're used to physical activity or not. It's suitable for any ability. There are three main types of stretches:

1. **Static.** With static stretches you hold a pose for at least 30-40 seconds which helps you develop greater flexibility and loosens muscles. In the past you may have been advised to bounce during static stretches but it's now known that this can cause injury. If you want a dynamic stretch try lunges or squats instead.

2. **Dynamic.** Dynamic stretches involve more body movement. Yoga is a good example of dynamic stretching.

3. **Pre-contraction.** This is a more advanced form of stretching that involves stretching and contracting specific muscle groups. If you want to try this, you are best off learning from an appropriately qualified coach.

You might like to incorporate stretching into your morning routine as a way to ease yourself into moving your body. A routine will help you consistently incorporate exercise into your daily life. Consistency is key to achieving long-lasting change.

When stretching, remember to warm up first. If you don't, you could hurt yourself. Even if you just do a few star jumps before you start to stretch, it will help you avoid injury. Take it slow and gradually build up your stretching. While increased flexibility is one of the positive effects of stretching, when you're doing it to improve your mental health, the practice is far more important than how bendy you are.

Here's some simple stretches you can start with:

1. **Forward fold.** Stand upright and soften your knees. Gradually bend forward, allowing your upper body to dangle loosely. Sway your body from side to side, releasing any tension in your lower back before gently rolling your body back up.

2. **Shoulder stretch.** Look straight ahead as you raise your arms above your head, palms facing up. Keep your arms aligned with your ears while you relax your shoulder blades. Hold your breath for five seconds. Roll your shoulders backwards and forwards and hold your breath for another five seconds.

3. **Foot stretch.** You might like to get a tennis ball for this exercise. Put it under your foot and shift your weight from the front of your foot to the back by rolling the ball forwards and backwards.

4. **Hip and knee stretch.** Hug one knee up to your chest. Hold your breath for five seconds. Now do this with the other leg.

However, there is more to yoga than stretching. It can be a very dynamic form of exercise as you move your body with the breath. You become more in tune with yourself. You may even find that some poses are highly challenging or even impossible when you first start. It can be deceptively difficult to maintain a balance or position.

But as my yoga teacher used to say, it's a yoga practice, not a yoga perfect. Over time, you will naturally become more limber and those poses that were hard at first become easier. Indeed, even within a single session, you can find yourself becoming more flexible as you breathe into a pose.

If possible, try to find a local yoga class to attend, at least while you get started. If you can't find one you like, there are many online options available, either live or pre-recorded. Alternatively, the poses below are a good starting point. Remember to always listen to your body and allow your moves to flow with your breath.

1.  **Mountain pose.** Stand straight with your feet together and your arms loosely hanging by your side. You might like to close your eyes as you find a strong, solid posture.

    You can stand like this for a few breaths or you can inhale as you lift your arms up and above your head to bring your palms together. Exhale and bring your hands down to your heart. Do a few cycles of this, inhaling to bring your arms above your head and then exhale, palms pressed together as they come back down to your heart.

2.  **Warrior one.** Sill in mountain pose, exhale and step your left foot back so you are lunging. Make sure your right knee is over your right ankle. Turn your left foot out slightly so it's at 45 degrees. Inhale and bring your arms straight above your head, palms facing each other. Keep your hips square and hold for a few breaths.

3.  **Warrior two.** Inhale, and as you exhale, lower your arms so that your right arm is pointing straight out in front of you and your left arm is pointing straight out behind you in a straight line. Keep your gaze forward and hold for a few breaths.

Now return to mountain pose and repeat warrior one and warrior two but stepping your right foot back this time.

4. **Cat/cow.** Move into a tabletop position on your hands and knees. Make sure your hands are beneath your shoulders and your knees below your hips with your spine in a neutral position. Inhale and lift up your head and tailbone slowly with the breath. Exhale and press into your hands as you lift your spine towards the sky, tucking your chin into your chest. Repeat this movement for a few cycles of breath, letting your breath guide you.

5. **Downward facing dog.** Return to your tabletop position. Have your palms beneath your shoulders, your knees beneath your hips, hip-width apart, and tuck your toes under. Lift your hips and push back into downward facing dog, making a V with your body. Try to get your feet flat on the floor but don't worry if you can't. You can gently pedal the feet to loosen up the hamstrings. Stay here for a few cycles of breath.

6. **Child's pose.** This is a beautiful resting position. Return to hands and knees. Bring your toes together, spreading the knees wide apart. Gently lower your butt down to your feet (or as far as it can go) and stretch your arms out in front of you. Try to have your forehead touching the floor, but if you can't get down that far, you can make fists with your hands and have your forehead rest against them. Stay here for as long as you need.

## ICE BATHS AND COLD SHOWERS

For me, Ice baths are where it all started.

*I'd love you to get into this. It's incredible!*

I'll never forget the feeling of climbing out of the ice that day. For starters, the incredible sense of achievement, of overcoming my fears of the cold. I felt alive in a way that I hadn't in years. Ice baths and cold water have been used since ancient times to treat a range of conditions. More recently, pioneers such as Wim Hof have brought hydrotherapy back into the mainstream to help people develop the resilience to deal with their challenges. While I was skeptical of how ice baths could help me recover from trauma, I'll admit that I was hooked from the very first time I plunged into that freezing water.

So how does it work?

It would appear that ice baths support healing by inducing the body's natural response to trauma. It is generally believed that cortisol is produced in response to acute stressors as a normal response to help deal with the situation. However chronically high levels of cortisol negatively impact on health causing issues such as obesity, inflammation and depression.[9]

Ice baths may help you process trauma by inducing the production of cortisol in the short term. This engenders various physiological reactions such as shivering, faster metabolism and raised heart rate, all of which can be the body's natural way of processing stress. It is entirely possible that immersing yourself in freezing water can normalize the production of cortisol, stimulating the body's natural healing functions. When the body shivers, it may be that this is enabling the nervous system to healthily flush the fight or flight energy built up during a traumatic event. Allowing this to occur may be a form of somatic healing that enables the whole being to recover from trauma.

## BREATHWORK

It's no accident that the lungs are the only organs in our body that we can consciously control. Humans have been using the breath to regulate everything from our mood to our body temperature for millennia. Countless studies have backed up what our ancestors knew - that the breath can help us heal all sorts of physical, mental, and emotional issues. It can lower our blood pressure, lower our heart rate, calm the mind, and ease the symptoms of trauma[10].

There are a range of different breathwork techniques available. If you go to yoga classes you may find that your teacher takes you through some as part of your practice. Alternatively, I outline some methods below.

Before you start working with the breath, it's important to be aware that it isn't appropriate for everyone. I would advise to consult a medical professional before you begin your practice, especially if you suffer from breathing complications or any of the following:

- **High blood pressure.** When using the breath for trauma work, you can experience some stressful emotions and memories which can elevate your blood pressure. If your blood pressure is already high, you are advised against breathwork.

- **Panic attacks or psychosis.** While breathwork can calm us when we're feeling anxious, for some people it can induce panic attacks, so it is best to start your practice under supervision from an appropriately trained professional.

- **Cardiovascular disease.** Some forms of breathwork can place strain on the heart if you have an existing cardiovascular problem.

- **Epilepsy.** If you are practicing rapid breathing as part of your breathwork practice, this can potentially trigger seizures.

- **Pregnancy.** Breathwork for trauma can raise your blood pressure and increase feelings of distress, which can be harmful for your baby.

## BOX BREATHING

Box breathing is a simple way of bringing your breath under control and calming you:

- Sit or lie down with your back supported and your airways clear.

- Close your eyes or unfocus your gaze.

- Inhale, counting to four in your mind.

- Hold the breath, counting to four in your mind.

- Exhale, counting to four in your mind.

- Hold the breath, counting to four in your mind.

Repeat for as long as you need.

## THE WIM HOF METHOD

This has been designed specifically to deal with trauma:

- Sit or lie down with your back supported and your airways clear.

- Close your eyes or unfocus your gaze.

- Inhale through the nose, allowing your belly to expand as you fully fill your lungs with air.

- Exhale through your mouth, completely emptying your lungs.

- Take 30-40 quick, powerful breaths, letting your abdomen lead the exhale. You may feel lightheaded or a tingling sensation. This is perfectly normal.

- When you are done, fully exhale.

- Inhale deeply, filling your lungs.

- Hold the air as long as possible.

- Take another big inhale, expanding your belly and chest.

- Hold this breath for 15 seconds then release.

- Repeat this cycle 3-4 times without taking a break between cycles.

## MOUTH BREATHING TECHNIQUE

- Set a timer for five minutes. As you become more familiar with this practice, you can increase the time you spend doing it to 10 or even 15 minutes.

- Lie flat on the floor with a straight spine to allow for the easy flow of air.

- Close your eyes.

- Inhale through your mouth, sending the air down to your belly.

- Inhale through your mouth again without exhaling, sending the air to your chest.

- Exhale through your mouth, making a sighing sound.

- Repeat this cycle until your alarm goes off.

- When you hear the alarm, release the mouth breathing and sit with however you're feeling for another five minutes.

- Let whatever thoughts or feelings come up to occur and allow yourself to observe them without judgment.

- After five minutes of sitting with yourself, open your eyes and return to your day.

If you find yourself crying or feeling physical sensations such as a tingling or panting, this is perfectly normal. You may also find your body temperature changes while you're mouth breathing.

You might like to journal about your experiences with breathwork to chart your progress.

## DIET

Rocket ships need rocket fuel. A healthy diet is essential to feeling good. Science is learning more and more about how what we eat affects all our health and not just our waistline. Sure, you can have pizza on a Friday night as an occasional treat, but if you make sure you eat plenty of fruit and vegetables during the week washed down with lots of water, you'll be supporting your mind and body to tackle life.

Just as they identified the power of water to heal, the Ancient Greeks understood the importance of a healthy diet. Hippocrates said "Let food be thy medicine." Since then, we've all known how important it is to eat well to maintain physical and mental wellbeing.

You don't need me to tell you what healthy food looks like. I think we all know that fruit and vegetables are good and processed foods are bad! What you may not know is just how bad unhealthy foods can be.

Sugar and processed food can cause inflammation throughout the body and brain. The irony is that it's precisely these 'comfort' foods that we reach for when we need to boost our mood, unwittingly making ourselves feel worse in the long run instead of better.

These foods are highly addictive and stimulate the production of feel-good dopamine. The only way to stop unhealthy cravings in their tracks is to stop eating those foods which will reprogram the brain to crave healthier alternatives.

It's so tempting to turn to a cup of coffee instead of breakfast though. (Which is why morning routines combined with an early start are so important!) We tend to go for convenience and when we're under stress, such as when we're dealing with trauma, we often eat too much or too little. We go for high-calorie fast foods instead of nourishing fruits and vegetables.

Science is becoming increasingly aware of the connection between gut health and mental health. It's a fascinating subject. Our gut has been described as the 'second brain' and it's linked to the brain via the vagus nerve which communicates signals that include how we should be feeling.[11]

Try to be more mindful about what you eat. This is so important that in your Workbook, we've added a simple food journal to track your eating habits. You may be surprised at what, where and when you eat and how closely this is linked to your trauma. If you discover you overeat when you feel stressed, you might like to take a moment to journal your feelings when you feel driven to stuff a cream cake down your throat to uncover what's really going on. If you're an under eater, you might want to break your meals down into five or six smaller ones instead of the traditional three main meals.

A healthy mind needs the right nutrients to support a healthy brain. You should be consuming a variety of foods instead of falling into a rut of eating the same things every day. Good brain foods include:

- Complex carbohydrates like brown rice and starchy vegetables to give you energy. These come with the added bonus of increased nutritional value, keeping you fuller for longer than the simple carbs found in sugar and candy.

- Lean proteins. These are another source of energy to improve cognitive function. Healthy sources include chicken, meat, fish, eggs, soybeans, nuts and seeds.

- Fatty acids. Found in fish, meat, eggs, nuts, and flaxseeds, these support brain function to promote better mental health.

- Water, water and more water. I try to drink a gallon a day. It's great for cleansing your bladder, enhancing brain function and raising energy levels. It can also be good for headaches if you sit in front of a computer all day, like I often do.

At the very least, try to eliminate processed foods from your diet. Stock up on healthy snacks you can have instead when you experience cravings.

Put together a healthy shopping list and stick to it. If you don't have any unhealthy foods in the house it'll be harder for you to fall back into old ways. Don't go shopping when you're hungry otherwise you may find yourself impulse buying comfort foods. Observe your food habits. If you've been eating in front of the TV, stop. This can make it easier for you to mindlessly overeat. Instead, be more mindful about your food. Eat at the table and truly focus on the sensation of putting food in your mouth, chewing it, and swallowing it..

## BOUNDARIES

Setting healthy boundaries may be a new concept to you, especially if you've fallen into people pleasing habits as a result of your trauma, but they're vital if you're going to manage your mental health.

'No' is a complete sentence. Get used to using it when you find yourself tempted to agree to something you don't want to do. Practice in front of the mirror so it doesn't seem so alien when you have to use it in real life. Role play if you feel it would be helpful.

In your Workbook, you'll be guided to brainstorm where you need to establish boundaries in your life. Where have you been saying yes when you should have been saying no? Where have you allowed other's needs to override your own?

Start putting your own needs first.

It's not selfish.

It's essential.

## DO WHAT YOU LOVE

Doing the things you love is highly therapeutic and lots of fun! We talked about inner child therapy in the last chapter. You're never too old to do what you love. Just because you're an adult doesn't mean you have to be all serious and stop enjoying yourself.

Make a list of things you love doing in your Workbook and make a promise to yourself you'll do at least one of them every day. The simple act of doing things that bring you joy will work wonders to elevate your mood and help you build a brighter world without trauma.

## LISTEN TO YOUR BODY AND REST

Possibly the most important lifestyle change you can make is to allow yourself rest. In our modern society we're pushed to be 'on' all the time, but this is counter productive in terms of allowing us to be our best selves. Associated with people pleasing is often hyper-independence and a belief that if I work hard and achieve everything I set out to I'll be a better person, but all this does is lead to burnout. When we let ourselves take time to rest and recover, we actually heal faster and achieve more with our time.

When we suffer a physical injury, we understand the importance of taking time out to heal. Yet we don't give ourselves the same kindness when it comes to mental trauma.

You'll find that going through therapy is *exhausting*. You may well make plans to do all your normal activities immediately after a session, but I'm warning you now: cancel them. You'll need to give yourself time to process whatever comes up during sessions. Likewise, if you've experienced an emotional release related to your trauma, you'll need to rest so you can assimilate your new understandings.

This is a journey that takes as long as it takes. You can't force it. The sooner you accept that, the faster you'll progress. You cannot underestimate how physically draining it is to heal from trauma and the effects can linger. Memories of abuse are stored in the body at a cellular level. When these are finally released, they also release toxins which will need to be processed.

You'll also feel mentally drained. When you've confronted a challenging issue, it's a shock to your system. Chances are you'll have learned something new about yourself and your response to trauma. You may well understand how you've been sabotaging yourself and why. It takes a lot of mental energy to cope with that.

Healing continues well beyond a therapy session. Once started, the body and mind continue with the process. This means that you may not experience breakthroughs until a few days after a session so you should be prepared to be kind to yourself as a consequence.

It might not seem like it, but you are doing a *lot* of hard work in processing your trauma. Sometimes your body will tell you that you need a break. Listen to it. If you don't, it may force you to take a break at the most inconvenient of times.

Remember that you are healing. You wouldn't force yourself to push through if you'd broken an arm or leg. So don't think you have to power through just because it's a mental issue and not so visible. Because you don't.

Be gentle with yourself, always.

Do yourself a favor. Schedule rest when you need it and make it non-negotiable. Your mind and body will thank you for it.

# CONCLUSION

## There Is No Destination

Recovering from trauma is not a race. There's no specific end goal. You're not going anywhere. Think of this process as walking a path without regard for where it's going to take you but with a strong interest in getting the thorn out of your shoe so you can enjoy every step.

Again: there is no goal. There's only the journey.

Your trauma happened. There's no way of changing that. You can't go back and change the past. But you can change the direction of your future.

You've learned all about how trauma has installed itself into every aspect of your existence. You've discovered all the ways trauma is preventing you from living life to its fullest.

You've also been given many tools to help you heal. You've been given an overview of the most popular types of therapy so you can make an informed choice over what direction to take. You've been provided with guidance to make simple yet powerful life choices to support your healing. Alongside all of this you've been provided with the Workbook filled with valuable exercises to keep you motivated and prepare for the pitfalls along the road.

What happens next is up to you.

I started my healing journey as a 51-year-old ex-drug addict. I'm confident that a successful journey can start wherever you may find yourself. I've been at the absolute bottom of the emotional pit, and I'm never going back there again. A life without trauma symptoms is possible and it's worth creating.

You deserve it.

You're worth it.

So make a choice *right now* that you will heal. It will take hard work and commitment but the rewards will far outweigh all of that.

I have faith in you. I'm proud of how far you've come and I know the rest of your journey will be magnificent.

Remember, you're not alone. I'm here, and there are others in the LearnWell Community, waiting to connect and continue growing alongside you.

Thank you so much for allowing me to share these thoughts with you. I would be profoundly moved to know that they have made a difference.

I hope our paths will cross one day. If they do, I'll spend the rest of that day listening to your amazing story.

I love you. You deserve to be happy.

Greg

# IN 90 SECONDS YOU CAN MAKE A HUGE DIFFERENCE

If you feel we've deserved it, please take a moment to leave a review on Amazon.

Your feedback means the world to us. It helps us to improve and it means better learning experiences for all our readers.

We'd be so grateful to you for your review!

Thank you!
Thank you!
Thank you!

# REFERENCES

## Introduction

1.  https://www.thenationalcouncil.org/wp-content/uploads/2022/08/Trauma-infographic.pdf

2.  https://www.ptsd.va.gov/understand/common/common_adults.asp

3.  https://www.brainline.org/article/how-ptsd-affects-brain

## Chapter One

1.  https://resourcecentre.savethechildren.net/pdf/vr59-01_protect_a_generation_report_en_0.pdf/

2.  https://reliefweb.int/report/world/covid-19-five-crises-facing-children-after-2-years-pandemic

3.  https://apibhs.com/2019/06/18/what-causes-some-people-and-not-other-to-develop-ptsd

## Chapter Two

1.  https://www.choosingtherapy.com/trauma-brain/

2.  https://www.health.harvard.edu/diseases-and-conditions/past-trauma-may-haunt-your-future-health

3.  https://pubmed.ncbi.nlm.nih.gov/31515885/

4.  https://evolutionnews.org/2018/11/memory-new-research-reveals-cells-have-it-too/

5.  https://www.frontiersin.org/articles/10.3389/fnbeh.2020.601939/full

6. https://www.sciencedaily.com/
   releases/2021/09/210922160651.htm

7. https://www.chcs.org/understanding-trauma-affects-
   health-health-care/

## Chapter Three

1. https://www.sciencedirect.com/science/article/abs/pii/
   S0165178119317834

2. https://pubmed.ncbi.nlm.nih.gov/19378696/

## Chapter Four

1. https://www.ncbi.nlm.nih.gov/books/NBK207191/

2. https://www.healthline.com/nutrition/gut-brain-
   connection#TOC_TITLE_HDR_2

3. https://www.engraciagill.com/trauma-tummy-trouble-6-
   ways-it-disrupts-your-gut/

4. https://www.sciencedirect.com/science/article/abs/pii/
   S0005791618301137?via%3Dihub

## Chapter Five

1. https://en.wikipedia.org/wiki/Strange_situation

2. https://www.psychologytoday.com/gb/blog/
   neuronarrative/201707/8-reasons-why-its-so-hard-really-
   change-your-behavior

3. https://albertellis.org/2015/06/all-or-nothing-thinking/

## Chapter Eight

1. https://www.psychiatrictimes.com/view/why-men-and-
   women-may-respond-differently-to-psychological-trauma

2. https://rehabs.com/pro-talk/how-relationships-regulate-our-nervous-system/#

## Chapter Ten

1. https://www.ncbi.nlm.nih.gov/pmc/articles/PMC4467776/

2. https://www.researchgate.net/profile/Sheila-Rauch/publication/226779802_Emotional_Processing_Theory_EPT_and_exposure_therapy_for_PTSD/links/5502e34d0cf2d60c0e64beb7/Emotional-Processing-Theory-EPT-and-exposure-therapy-for-PTSD.pdf

3. https://www.ptsd.va.gov/professional/treat/txessentials/cpt_for_ptsd_pro.asp

4. https://www.ncbi.nlm.nih.gov/pmc/articles/PMC6224348/

5. https://slate.com/technology/2015/07/prolonged-exposure-therapy-for-ptsd-the-vas-treatment-has-dangerous-side-effects.html

6. https://www.frontiersin.org/articles/10.3389/fpsyt.2022.804491/full

7. https://med.nyu.edu/departments-institutes/population-health/divisions-sections-centers/medical-ethics/education/high-school-bioethics-project/learning-scenarios/ptsd-treatment-psychedelics

8. https://maps.org/mdma/ptsd/

9. https://www.ncbi.nlm.nih.gov/pmc/articles/PMC5518443/

10. https://www.ptsduk.org/emotional-freedom-therapy/

11. https://www.reiki.org/articles/reiki-hospitals

## Chapter Eleven

1. https://onlinelibrary.wiley.com/doi/abs/10.1002/hec.1389

2. https://www.ncbi.nlm.nih.gov/pmc/articles/PMC3630977/

3. https://www.ncbi.nlm.nih.gov/pmc/articles/PMC3830620/

4. https://mindworks.org/blog/physical-mental-benefits-of-meditation/

5. https://www.webmd.com/mental-health/features/meditation-ptsd

6. https://europepmc.org/article/med/15518309

7. https://academic.oup.com/brain/article/137/5/1514/333397

8. https://www.vantagefit.io/blog/mental-benefits-of-stretching/

9. https://www.morozkoforge.com/post/ice-bath-trauma-ptsd

10. https://www.othership.us/resources/breathwork-benefits

11. https://hms.harvard.edu/news-events/publications-archive/brain/gut-brain

Made in the USA
Monee, IL
11 June 2026

53148714R00115